The World of Wallace & Gromit

WEST WALLABY STREET

First published 2004 by Boxtree
an imprint of Pan Macmillan Ltd
Pan Macmillan, 20 New Wharf Road, London N1 9RR
Basingstoke and Oxford
Associated companies throughout the world
www.panmacmillan.com

ISBN 0 7522 1558 2

Produced under license by Aardman Animations
© and ™ Aardman/Wallace & Gromit Ltd 2004
www.aardman.com

Text © Aardman Animations Ltd 2004

Photographs: pp.123-4 © Glico & Daiko Advertising;
p.125 © Hakahodo; pp.16, 126–7 © Renault; p.129 ©
Jacobs & Euro RSCG; pp.130–2, 137 © Simon
Richardson & Mark Douet; pp.170–1, 173 © Neospace;
p.172 © @t-Bristol.
All other images © Aardman Animations Ltd.

9 8 7 6 5 4 3 2 1

A CIP catalogue record for this book is available from
the British Library.

Designed by Dan Newman, Perfect Bound Ltd
Colour Reproduction by Aylesbury Studios (Bromley) Ltd
Printed and bound in Great Britain by The Bath Press

Aardman
presents

The World of Wallace & Gromit

Andy Lane

BOXTREE

Contents

Foreword   6

Introduction   8

How is it all done?   14

The characters   18

'Hold tight lad, and think of Lancashire hotpot' 38
   A Grand Day Out

'There goes my knotted pine'   56
   The Wrong Trousers

'The bounce has gone from his bungee'   78
   A Close Shave

'The Edam is stranded!'   100
Wallace & Gromit's Cracking Contraptions

'It's Apocalypse Chow!'   122
Wallace & Gromit go global

'Gromit makes a smashing camel!'   130
Wallace & Gromit Alive on Stage
in A Grand Night Out

'The penguin is mightier than the sword'   138
Wallace & Gromit take on Project Zoo

'An absurd chap, in the position of Cary Grant'   144
The music

'Don't forget, you can't write charm'   148
Getting the voices right

'Where are Wallace & Gromit?'   152
A close shave in New York

'Liable to be swayed by a penguin'   162
Why do we love Wallace & Gromit so much?

'Can I have a break?'   174
The future for Wallace & Gromit
Credits   180
Film festivals and awards   183
Acknowledgements   184

Contents

Foreword

I'm often asked what the secret is to Wallace and Gromit, and why they appeal to such a wide range of ages. I'm never really sure I know the answer completely. It's hard to commentate on your own work. It's obviously got something to do with the characters. The thoughtless stupidity of Wallace in contrast to his much more intelligent and sensitive pooch, and the way the plasticine medium allows them to express themselves in a very reserved and peculiarly British way, especially in the eyebrows, and also the held-back, understated humour of the stories.

But these are things I observe in retrospect. Things that people tell me. What I find hardest to pin down, is exactly where ideas come from and how the Wallace and Gromit stories come about. All I know is that I love to make people laugh. I've been fortunate enough to have had the right elements and the right people coming together at the right time to provide the ideal vehicle to carry off my ideas. People like Peter Sallis with his unique and endearing voice; animators like Steve Box and all those who can breathe life and humour into plasticine; talented and funny writers like Bob Baker; cinematographers like Dave Alex Riddett and Tristan Oliver, good editors, art department, set designers, model makers, Julian Nott's music scores; Adrian Rhodes' sound and mixing. These people, each in their discipline, bring character and style to the whole.

'Won't you come in? We were just about to have some cheese.'

I often find myself, in looking for ways forward, listening and learning from what they and others tell me about the characters and their world. They may be right or they may be wrong, but it's as if the first adventure, *A Grand Day Out*, offered a glimpse into a bigger, already existing world that I'm still not yet fully aware of. It's then I get a sense that the stories and characters are really writing themselves or, more accurately, being written by Wallace and Gromit themselves.

So this book is for Wallace and Gromit and all those who have helped shape, in so many senses, their characters and their world.

Nick Park
June 2004

Introduction

There aren't many fictional characters who have their own cheese. There's no James Bond Cheddar ('licensed to melt gently over your toast'), nor a Harry Potter Stilton ('the magic's in the mould!'). There is, however, a Wallace and Gromit Wensleydale ('the official Wallace & Gromit cheese' according to the Wensleydale dairy products website – presumably in order to discourage all those unofficial Wallace and Gromit cheeses flooding the market). This immediately sets Wallace and Gromit apart from other world-famous fictional characters. They're eccentric. They're idiosyncratic. They're British through and through, and proud of it. They're extraordinary, without realizing it. And, it goes without saying that, unlike the cheese that bears their name, they're made of plasticine.

Nick Park, the man behind their phenomenal success, is an unlikely player in the highly competitive film and TV industry. A quietly spoken Lancastrian with an endearing habit of forgetting what he was saying halfway through a sentence, he was brought up watching stop-motion animated children's series such as *The Clangers* (1969–74) and *Bagpuss* (1974). Knowing that he wanted to make the same kind of programmes himself, he first went to art school and then took a course in animation at the National Film and Television School in the early 1980s.

Nick created the bald inventor Wallace and his intelligent dog Gromit as part of his graduation project, using stop-motion techniques that had been around since the turn of the century, but the film wasn't finished when he completed his course. Following his graduation, Nick joined Aardman Animations – a company created by Peter Lord and David Sproxton, and best known for the success of the diminutive plasticine character Morph – and spent some years alternatively working on Morph and various commercials for Aardman while trying to finish the Wallace and Gromit film in his spare time. Realizing that progress was painfully slow, even for animation, Peter Lord and David Sproxton offered to let Nick finish the film on company time.

That first Aardman production to star Wallace and Gromit – *A Grand Day Out* (1990) – told the story of how the two eccentrics run out of cheese and decide to pop out to replenish the cupboard. Of course, given Wallace's tendency to complicate even the simplest of issues, he decides that the best place to get cheese from is the Moon, rather than the local corner shop. So he builds a rocket (or, rather, Gromit builds a rocket for him) and they set off. Things never go quite to plan in the world of Wallace and Gromit, however, and they have to escape the clutches of a coin-operated alien robot before they can return for supper.

The second TV film, *The Wrong Trousers* (1994), is a more parochial affair, tying the two inventors into an Ealing comedy-like farce involving robberies and false identities. Wallace's newest acquisition – a pair of automatic trousers that will save him the labour of actually walking Gromit himself – are hijacked by a criminal penguin who is lodging with them. The penguin uses the trousers (and Wallace!) to continue his crime spree around the local area, but Gromit is wise to his game, and decides to bring the avian thief to justice.

'Tell you what, Gromit lad, let's have a nice hot cup of tea.'

9

In the third of the TV films, *A Close Shave* (1995), Wallace has turned his inventing talents toward the window-cleaning business. While Gromit risks life and tail in Wallace's contraption, the eccentric inventor meets Wendolene – proprietress of the local wool shop – and her dog, Preston. Gromit suspects Preston of having connections to a sheep-rustling ring, but Wallace has fallen for Wendolene's comfortable, cardigan-clad charms and cannot believe that she could be involved in something as heinous as sheep-rustling. The pair investigate, but soon discover that Wallace isn't the only inventor in the neighbourhood ...

Wallace and Gromit took England by storm when *A Grand Day Out* first appeared on television in 1990, and the fame of the plasticine pair has spread worldwide since then. Both *The Wrong Trousers* and *A Close Shave* won Nick Park the Academy Award for best animated film (he'd already won the same award for his first real piece of work at Aardman – *Creature Comforts* (1989) – and been nominated for *A Grand Day Out* at the same time in the same category).

Despite the fact that *A Grand Day Out* was first shown in 1990, and that the three films get the occasional airing at Christmas but little else, people still recognize the eccentric, cheese-loving inventor and the dog with the expressive forehead. Pop into any branch of a popular car parts dealership and

Above: Wendolene is shocked to discover that Wallace has substituted a chunk of cheese for the traditional Sunday roast. Opposite: 'Feathers' McGraw is delivered to the local constabulary in The Wrong Trousers.

you can fill your basket with Wallace and Gromit car mats and nodding figures for the back seat. Visit your local supermarket and, chances are, you'll find the Wallace and Gromit Wensleydale cheese.

'Gromit, that's it — cheese! We'll go somewhere where there's cheese!'

Recognizing that the plasticine pair had joined that pantheon of characters who had transcended their origins, along with James Bond, Sherlock Holmes and various original Disney creations like Mickey Mouse and Donald Duck, Aardman took the surprising decision *not* to base their first feature film around them, even though it would have guaranteed a worldwide fan base. *Chicken Run* (2000), bankrolled by Hollywood and successful across the globe, proved that Aardman could make it big using completely new characters. Having sorted that out to their own satisfaction, they then returned to the clay companions and started production on the first cinema outing for Wallace and Gromit – tentatively entitled *Wallace & Gromit Curse of the WereRabbit* and scheduled for a 2005 release.

Wallace's eccentric inventing skills have also been explored in a series of ten short films. *Wallace & Gromit's Cracking Contraptions* (2002) is a guide to the bizarre ways that Wallace finds to occupy his time. There's the Snoozatron, the

Snowmanatron and the Soccamatic machine, as well as the Bullyproof Vest and the Tellyscope. The films – each less than two minutes in length, premiered on the Internet, and should help keep the public entertained until *Wallace & Gromit Curse of the WereRabbit* is finished.

Other spin-offs along the way have provided more of an insight into the world of Wallace and Gromit. There have been comic strips and books devoted to their activities, and there's even a computer game, but despite their ubiquity they are unique, and somehow isolated. The two of them seem to inhabit their own world, far away from everything and everyone else, a world that's simpler than ours and yet verging much more towards the surreal. A world in which people think nothing of flying to the Moon for cheese.

A world, let's be honest, in which most of us would much rather live.

Above: The terrifying metallic figure of Preston menaces our heroes in A Close Shave.

Left: Gromit's penchant for active sports is likely to be foiled by the weight of Wallace's cast iron skis.

How is it all done?

Wallace and Gromit aren't actors. Hopefully that shouldn't come as a shock to anyone reading this book. They're made of plasticine – a mixture of clay, oil and pigment. Very simple ingredients.

And yet, in a strange way, they *are* real. They have character, they have personality, and we actually believe – at least, for the time they are on our TV screens – that they exhibit real emotions.

How do we explain this discrepancy? How can two small piles of modelling clay convince us that they are as real as we are? The answer is something called 'stop-motion animation', and it's something that Aardman Animations – the company responsible for all of Wallace and Gromit's adventures – specializes in.

The technique of stop-motion animation has been around for nearly a century – almost as long as films themselves. In essence, it's simple – so simple that it can be done on a kitchen table (which, oddly enough, is where David Sproxton and Peter Lord began the process that led to their founding Aardman Animations).

Ordinary films are a series of still pictures taken at a rate of about twenty four shots per second. When projected back at this rate, they give the impression of movement. The key to understanding stop-motion animation is the realization that the pictures don't have to be taken at the rate at which they are going to be shown. You could take a picture of a ball of clay, then mould it slightly, take another picture, mould it a bit more, take another picture, and so on. Eventually you might have, say, 240 photographs, the first one of which shows a ball of clay and the last of which shows a small man made of clay. Taking those photographs might have occupied you for the best part of a day. Project the pictures one after the other at the standard rate of twenty four pictures per second and you have a ten-second film showing a ball of clay transforming itself into a small man. Easy!

In fact, what you have, actually, is Morph – the character invented by David Sproxton and Peter Lord who made his first appearance on the BBC children's series *Take Hart* and who went on to get his own series, *The Amazing Adventures of Morph* (1981).

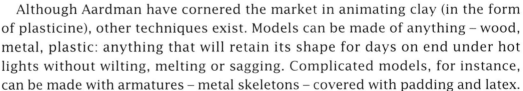

Opposite: Morph poses in front of his own clapperboard.
Above: Nick Park works on Wallace and Gromit.

Although Aardman have cornered the market in animating clay (in the form of plasticine), other techniques exist. Models can be made of anything – wood, metal, plastic: anything that will retain its shape for days on end under hot lights without wilting, melting or sagging. Complicated models, for instance, can be made with armatures – metal skeletons – covered with padding and latex.

'All different materials have their pros and cons,' says Debbie Smith, a model-maker who has been with Aardman for many years. 'Plasticine is something that you can poke and it won't change, whereas clay will dry out. Wood and metal are really hard work to try and change. You can get something modelled up very quickly in plasticine. The disadvantage is that you can't make it permanent. But then you don't want it permanent for animation.'

Oddly, although people assume that Wallace and Gromit are both made entirely of plasticine, various parts of Wallace are actually solid. His green tank top is usually cast in resin or plastic, giving the animators something solid to hold, and his slippers and legs might be made of foam. The only parts that *have* to be made of plasticine are the parts which need to move – his face, his mouth, his arms and hands. Gromit is a different matter, however. He doesn't wear tank tops or slippers, so there's nowhere to hide any joins between plasticine and whatever other materials might be used. Gromit, for that reason, is entirely plasticine apart from his eyes and nose which, like

Above: Setting Gromit up
for a shot in the Renault
Kangoo advert.
Left: Checking the shot on
the monitor.

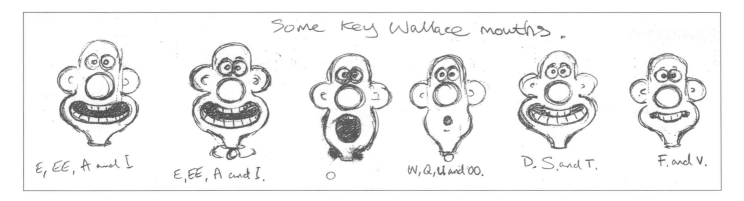

Some key Wallace mouths.

E, EE, A and I.   E, EE, A and I.   O   W, Q, U and OO.   D. S. and T.   F. and V.

Above: Wallace can be fitted with a mouth for every occasion, or at least every sound he makes. Below: Gromit, who has no mouths – spare or otherwise.

Wallace's eyes, are simple beads, and an internal armature to give him some rigidity.

Mouths are the trickiest part. When Wallace first appeared in *A Grand Day Out*, his animator – Nick Park – sculpted every movement of his mouth to match the dialogue that had been pre-recorded by Peter Sallis. In later films a more inventive technique was used whereby a series of different mouths were made for different sounds ('eee', 'oooh', 'aaah' and so on), and the mouths were swapped over to match what Peter Sallis was saying on a syllable-by-syllable basis.

The model-makers at Aardman have got the process of constructing these figures down to a fine art, which is useful considering the number of models they end up making ...

'I can knock up a rough Wallace or Gromit in a day,' says Debbie, 'but if you've got a complex armature inside, obviously it takes longer. It depends how neat and tidy you want it. You can spend up to a week on something and I don't know that it would actually be any better on the fifth day than on the second or third.'

Making the models and animating them is really only part of the process. They also have to be put into context. Wallace has his house, Wendolene has her shop, and there are other places (like the Moon or the local museum) that get visited from time to time. All of these sets have to be built from scratch, and built to such an exacting requirement that they look absolutely real, even though they might only be a few feet across. Then they have to be lit. It's a complicated process, putting Wallace and Gromit through their paces, and behind the animator stand an entire team of people who have contributed their own particular skills.

Stop-motion animation is something between an art and a craft. It requires immense patience and vision, as well as a highly developed sense of body language and movement, but ultimately it's understandable. Achievable. People feel, rightly or wrongly, that given a ball of clay and a film camera they could probably do it themselves. And that's part of the very special charm of Wallace and Gromit – we feel comfortable with them.

But that's only part of their story. Explaining the rest will take a bit of doing ...

How is it all done?

The characters

What do we know about Wallace, apart from his cheerful optimism, his fondness for cheese and his ability to cobble together an invention for any purpose? What do we know about Gromit, his faithful friend and companion, apart from the fact that he acts as the long-suffering test subject for his master's creations? Actually, over the course of their adventures we've found out a surprising amount about them and, in passing, about a few of the other denizens of their world ...

Wallace

'I do a bit of that myself,' says Wallace in *A Close Shave* when Wendolene Ramsbottom tells him that her father was an inventor. He's not kidding. Wallace is a regular one-man research laboratory, working out of the basement of his terraced house and producing labour-saving devices that are just that little bit too complicated, and just that little bit too unsafe, to make his fortune. His best friend – in fact, possibly his only friend – is his dog, Gromit, who acts as the counterbalance to Wallace's wild optimism and sudden switches in attention. Together they form an inseparable team, one that's equally as likely to be travelling to the Moon as to the local corner shop.

'My name is Wallace. People call me ... Wallace.'

It's hard to believe Wallace could live anywhere apart from the place in which he was born and bred: a small town in Lancashire. He is a true Northerner, in speech as well as in dress sense. He wears baggy trousers, shirts that resemble pyjama jackets, tank tops, and probably has a raincoat and a bobble hat for when its windy. He also demonstrates that particular form of directness that manifests itself in Northern folk: there's no mucking about with Wallace, he'll call a spade a spade (and probably redesign it as an all-terrain, multi-purpose digging utensil whilst he's at it).

Wallace lives where he's probably lived all his life: 62 West Wallaby Street. Externally it's a red brick, terraced house with a well-kept garden, but inside it's a revelation! Years of renovation and redecoration have resulted in the house appearing surprisingly larger than it should be. The basement area has, at different times, provided enough space for

a Moon rocket launch pad, a sheep-shearing area and an expansive work space, while the walls are largely hollowed out in order to accommodate the vast amount of machinery that Wallace has created to make his life more comfortable. In fact, it's entirely possible that the house is just one vast machine that happens to be decorated with wallpaper and a lick of paint!

Overleaf: Nick Park's early plans for constructing one man and his dog.

Wallace's greatest pleasures in life are inventing and cheese. Inventing is what he does best. Actually, it's what he does incessantly, all day every day, when he's not sitting down with a cup of tea and a plate of cheese and crackers. Things to make his life better, things to make the world better, things that just seemed like a good idea at the time – he'll turn his hand to anything. One of his areas of speciality is robots: he's designed them to cook food, clean the house, build sandcastles and head down to the shops for him. Another area in which he excels is transport: having built everything from a motorcycle-sidecar combination to a Moon-rocket, via an autogyro made from a converted bathtub.

For a man who expends such vast amounts of energy in building his inventions, Wallace is surprisingly lazy. He loves to lie in bed and snooze, but he hates to get up, so he built a device that allows him to slide out of bed, through a hole in his bedroom floor and into a chair at the kitchen table, cleverly falling into his clothes while doing so. He loves to eat but is too lazy to cook, so he has made several attempts to construct machines that will produce a full English breakfast at the press of a button. He loves sport but he hates physical exercise, so he put together a creation that can fire footballs at a goal without any human intervention. Ironically, of course, he expends more energy building these labour-saving contraptions than he would in actually doing the work in the first place.

Wallace's lifestyle is surprisingly simple. When he's not building something in the basement, he just likes to sit and read the local paper. His best friend is his dog, Gromit, and the two of them are perfectly happy together. Every now and then someone else will cross their paths – a psychotic penguin, an inventor's daughter with a cheese allergy, a robot dog with a penchant for mutton pies – but nothing dents the perfect domestic respectability of the duo for long.

The World of Wallace & Gromit

If Wallace has one passion, it's cheese. He loves the stuff. Gorgonzola, Wensleydale, Stilton, Camembert ... Wallace isn't fussy: he'll eat the lot, spread on nice, crisp crackers and with a decent cup of tea by his side. He even has a subscription to *Cheese Holidays* magazine, allowing him to plan a whole succession of cheese-related trips. His rocket ship, built in the basement beneath the house, was constructed solely so that he and Gromit could get to the Moon and replenish their cheese supplies. Obsession might be too strong a word, but Wallace certainly loves his cheese.

'Ooh, I do like a bit of gorgonzola.'

Despite the fact that he and Gromit have lived together for as long as Wallace cares to remember, he can be surprisingly careless about the pooch's feelings. When Wallace decided that they needed a lodger in to help pay the bills, for instance, Gromit quickly felt marginalized and ended up moving out of the house, but Wallace just kept on paying attention to the new penguin in the house. Similarly, when Wallace fell for wool-shop owner Wendolene Ramsbottom, he completely failed to notice that Gromit saw this as a threat to their cosy domestic relationship. No, Wallace may be many things, but he's not good at emotions.

Having said that, Wallace is loyal to a fault. Following Gromit's arrest and subsequent incarceration for sheep-stealing (a charge trumped up by evil robot dog Preston) Wallace risked his own freedom by breaking Gromit out of jail. He was quite prepared to help smuggle Gromit to freedom abroad, but instead helped the mutt to clear his name. He always remembers Gromit's birthday – although his choice of gifts often leaves something to be desired – and he always managed to find a place for Gromit in his schemes, plans and excursions. Wallace without Gromit would be ... well, it would be like cheese without crackers!

CHARACTER SHEET ①
(MATERIALS)

MAYBE USE ~~A~~ READY-MADE LEG POSITIONS CYCLE
FOR REPETIVE WALKING ACTION.

MADE of CLAY or 'DAS'
(CYCLE of 16?)

CHANGE BACK TO PLASTICENE LEGS WHEN MAN IS STATIC OR ~~MOVING~~ DIFFERENT ACTION.

...E TOTALLY of PLASTICENE EXCEPT for NOSE.

Gromit

A dispassionate observer, watching 62 West Wallaby Street from afar, might have trouble in working out who was in charge.

On the face of it, Wallace should be the master. He's taller, he can talk and he's human. Gromit, by contrast, is short, mute and canine (not usually attributes associated with someone in a position of authority). On the other hand, when something goes wrong in the household (which it often does) who is it that usually saves the day? Gromit, of course. When Wallace comes up with yet another hare-brained, badly thought through plan, who is it who raises his eyebrows and tries to get the whole thing back on a more rational footing? Gromit, that's who. And when villains need confronting, evil penguins require chastising and robot dogs deserve a good thrashing, who steps forward without hesitation? We'll leave you to guess.

Above: Gromit waits in vain for someone to hit his conker.

Gromit has many characteristics that make him the perfect foil to Wallace. Where Wallace is enthusiastic, Gromit is practical. Where Wallace is optimistic, Gromit injects a note of realism. Where Wallace's head is often turned by a plausible lodger or an attractive inventor's daughter, Gromit always stays loyal to his master. Even if it's three o'clock in the morning and Wallace can't get

Above: Wallace and Gromit demonstrate the speedy response of their window cleaning service in A Close Shave.
Opposite below: Gromit's position as Wallace's faithful companion is usurped by a fiendish penguin in The Wrong Trousers.
Right and overleaf: Nick's sketches of Gromit.

to sleep, Gromit will climb into a woolly costume and bounce through a trapdoor into Wallace's bedroom so that Wallace can count sheep and get back to sleep, and all this with nothing more than a glower and a scowl.

There must be times when Gromit wonders if he's properly appreciated in the household. Perhaps he thinks he gets taken for granted. But he loves Wallace, despite Wallace's bizarre obsessions, and it would take a lot to make him leave. On the one occasion where he's ever actually packed his bags and left, when his place in the house was supplanted by the superficially plausible 'Feathers' McGraw, he was so lonely and so worried about Wallace that he had to come back. And good thing too, for the evil criminal penguin had used Gromit's absence to take control of 62 West Wallaby Street and use it as the basis for a fiendishly clever plan to steal a diamond from the local museum!

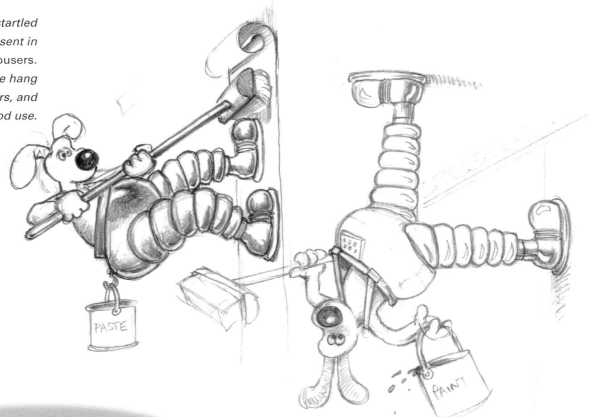

Opposite: Gromit is startled by his birthday present in The Wrong Trousers.
Right: He soon got the hang of the techno-trousers, and put them to good use.

'Cracking toast, Gromit!'

Whereas Wallace is an improvisational inventor, building his bizarre contraptions out of whatever comes to hand, Gromit is more of an intellectual. When he's not taking part in his master's life-threatening schemes, he can usually be found curled up in a chair reading a book. He's very fond of literature – *Crime and Punishment* by Fido Dogstoyevsky is a particular favourite – but often tries to improve his mind with a science textbook such as *Electronics for Dogs* or a philosophical tract like Pluto's *The Republic*.

Gromit is a genuine hero. When danger threatens his master, he immediately leaps into action without a thought for his own safety. On the occasion when 'Feathers' McGraw was forcing Wallace to steal a diamond for him, it was Gromit who not only uncovered the plan but confronted the penguin, chased him through the house despite a hail of gunfire and eventually captured him in a milk bottle. The time a robot dog was about to feed Wallace, his friend Wendolene and a flock of sheep into a mincing machine, it was Gromit who rescued the hostages, confronted the malevolent machine and (with the help of one of the sheep) made sure that he got pushed into the terrible rotating jaws of the machine instead. And when a whole group of animals from the local zoo, including his friend Archie the Polar Bear, were imprisoned by the wicked penguin and used as slave labour in an attempt to mine diamonds, it was Gromit who kicked and punched his way through the various levels of the zoo, fighting the penguin's nasty cohorts until he could rescue them. Gromit has no fears for his own safety: he confronts evil wherever he finds it and biffs it on the nose.

Shaun

There's something about Shaun the Sheep that makes him stand out from the rest of his flock. Something that sets him apart. Even the rest of the sheep have difficulty telling one from another, but they all know Shaun. He's smaller than the rest, for one thing – more of a lamb than a sheep. He's also much more curious. The others would quite happily stand in a field all day, come rain or shine, eating the grass and commenting to each other on the patterns the clouds make in the sky, but Shaun always wanted to know what was beyond the fence, or over the hill, or down the end of the lane and round the corner.

When the entire flock was stolen by the evil robot dog Preston and his helpless owner Wendolene, the other sheep just went along for the ride. They weren't happy about it, but they weren't about to make trouble. Shaun, however, showed another character trait that distinguished him from his friends – his courage. Taking advantage of the generally shoddy workmanship in Preston's van, he escaped through a hole in the

Above: Shaun has yet to get to grips with the concept of carol singing. Still, at least he comes in on the right baaa.

The World of Wallace & Gromit

Above: A typical English May Day celebration. Opposite and right: Shaun demonstrates his wooly jumper, both before and after it passed through Wallace's Knit-O-Matic in A Close Shave.

'The little chap must be really hungry.'

side when the van was stationary at a set of traffic lights in West Wallaby Street and trotted to safety inside Number 62, watched by the rest of his friends – and by Preston the robot dog.

Pretty quickly, Shaun demonstrated to Wallace – the man whose house he had wandered into – yet another point of difference between him and the other sheep. His appetite. Shaun will eat anything. Cheese, potted plants, newspapers, electrical flex: nothing is safe from his grinding, ruminant teeth. He'll eat and keep on eating until he's actually physically prevented from eating any more. And nobody knows where he puts it all! It's not like he's growing any fatter! In fact, Wallace is pretty convinced that somewhere inside Shaun lies the long-sought secret of perpetual digestion.

'Feathers' McGraw

'Feathers' McGraw. It's a name that strikes fear into the hearts of law-abiding citizens across the entire North of England. Long thought to be a chicken of criminal mien, McGraw was actually exposed as a penguin with a rubber glove on his head when his plan to rob a museum of a precious diamond was foiled by a local inventor and his trusty canine sidekick.

'Feathers' McGraw's greatest asset is his imperturbability. Cool, collected and not easily worried, he regularly uses his razor keen intellect to come up with complicated plans which he is then able to execute without the slightest sign of nerves. His speciality is insinuating himself into a respectable household and setting up a base of operations, somehow involving the occupants in his schemes as unwitting, or unwilling, accomplices.

'Feathers' is an expert technician, and his schemes frequently depend on complicated devices of one kind or another. Quick on the uptake, the penguin is a dab hand with a spanner and a soldering iron. He also has no qualms about handling a gun, and if cornered he is likely to attempt to shoot his way out of trouble.

Following his ambitious attempt to relieve the local museum of its gemstone treasure, 'Feathers' was incarcerated in the local zoo. He wasn't there for long, however. Breaking out, he then proceeded to break back in again and blackmail the rest of the animals into taking part in a

Opposite: 'Feathers' McGraw arrives in 62 West Wallaby Street.
Above: Within a short time, the penguin had inveigled himself into Wallace's good graces.

complicated scheme to create diamonds from ice and coal. He built himself a little empire deep in the bowels of the zoo, but once again it was Wallace, the local inventor, and his faithful pooch Gromit who uncovered and foiled his plans.

Above: 'Feathers' McGraw never missed a chance to cause trouble.
Right: Wallace and Wendolene first realised their feelings for one another when their hands met over a ball of wool.

Wendolene

Wendolene Ramsbottom is not what one might call the most glamorous of women. Her wardrobe runs more to cardigans and skirts than designer dresses, and her hairstyle appears to have been based on a motorcycle helmet. She looks like she should be running a stall selling marmalade at a Women's Institute fair, not rustling sheep in the dead of night. Appearances, however can be deceiving.

'Of all the women that I've met ... Not that I've met many you understand.'

Wendolene's father was a noted local inventor. When he died, Wendolene found herself in reduced circumstances, and was forced to open a small wool shop and try to earn a meagre living. Despite her father's success, all he ended up leaving her was his last invention – a robotic dog named Preston. He had designed Preston to look after Wendolene, but little did he know what was to come.

All Wendolene really wants is a quiet life, but Preston has other ideas. Intimidating her with his imposing physical strength and appearance, he forces her to help him in a scheme to steal sheep from the local area in order to obtain cheap wool for her shop. It is Preston's way of staying true to his programming to look after Wendolene, but she doesn't see it that way. Frightened of Preston's sharp, metallic teeth, she goes along with his plans. Her wool shop prospers – as well it might, given that it is now the only source of wool for miles around – but Wendolene suddenly becomes aware that Preston has other plans. Shocked at her discovery that he intends to turn the stolen sheep into pies, Wendolene finds within herself an unexpected reserve of moral courage, but it is almost too late. Preston finally overcomes the last remnants of his programming and attempts to feed

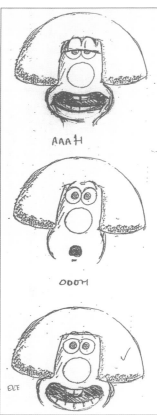

Wendolene into the mincing machine with the sheep and local inventor and
window cleaner Wallace, but they are all rescued at the last moment by a dog
named Gromit and a sheep named Shaun.

Although Wendolene has developed strong feelings for Gromit's master,
Wallace, the shame she feels at the way she has been used means that she
cannot tell him how she feels. And her cheese allergy means that the two of
them can never be compatible. So Wendolene is left, alone, to run her wool
shop and wait for her windows to get so dirty that she can give Wallace a
ring and ask him to come over.

Preston

Preston was designed to make life easier for Wendolene Ramsbottom
and her father, but he developed and grew, becoming hungry for
power. Eventually he has come to dominate the rather meek
Wendolene, and involves her in his schemes to steal sheep from
the local farmers. Initially Preston was just trying to help
Wendolene with her wool business by providing extra balls of wool
for her shop, but he quickly came to realise that the by-product of
the sheering – sheared sheep – could be used for other purposes. For
instance, making dog food.

Preston used to be a brutal, unpleasant creature. Shrewd without being
particularly far-sighted, he could instantly size up a situation and turn it

*Opposite: Weldolene loves roses. So does Shaun, but for different reasons.
Below: Preston's baleful glance was enough to scare anyone he looked at.
Right: Stripped of his artificial skin, Preston wasn't just scary – he was terrifying!*

to his advantage. He relied on his overbearing strength to allow him to get his way in any situation, and he didn't like to be crossed. Having identified Gromit as a potential problem, he quickly set about bullying the poor mutt and eventually framed him for a crime he did not commit.

Beneath Preston's short-haired, heavily muscled exterior lay a metallic skin, and beneath that a mass of gears, cogs and levers. He was completely automatic, with no canine components at all. Following a fortunate accident in a mincing machine, Preston was completely redesigned by Wallace into a much more pleasing, and much less dangerous form. Now he is perfectly capable of fetching the paper in the morning, but much less likely to commit heinous crimes.

'Hold tight lad, and think of Lancashire hotpot'
A Grand Day Out

Part of the charm of *A Grand Day Out* – directed by Nick Park and produced under the aegis of Aardman Animations – is the uncertain world in which it exists: a world in which an inventor can decide to travel to the Moon in order to replenish his larder, accompanied only by a dog who helped him build his rocket in the first place. One can't help wondering if everyone in West Wallaby Street is as strange as Wallace; everyone in Northern England; everyone on Nick Park's Earth. Or is it just Wallace?

Nobody had seen anything quite like *A Grand Day Out* before its premier on Channel 4 on Christmas Eve, 1990. Stop-motion animation was nothing particularly special on TV, of course: we'd had Morph, the animated plasticine figure who had appeared in *Take Hart*, as well as things like *The Trap Door* (1985), *The Wombles* (1974 and 1998) and *The Magic Roundabout* (1965–77 and 1992), but they were very definitely for kids. And we'd had the various Aardman late-night stop-motion one-offs shown on Channel 4 under the overall umbrella titles of *Conversation Pieces* (1983) and *Lip Synch* (1989), along with the claymation films of Jan Svankmajer, but they were closer to video art than anything else. *A Grand Day Out* was something new: a short film with a plot and a sense of humour, aimed at all the family and produced with what amounted to cinematic lighting and editing. It was a step up from anything that had been done before.

Another part of its charm is, paradoxically, its crudeness. Most stop-motion animation aims to be as clean and neat as possible, but Nick Park in *A Grand Day Out* actually made a virtue of the fact that fingerprints appear in the plasticine. It looks worked, rather than being perfect. It looks like something a craftsman has produced, rather than a factory. And that, in the end, is what attracted people to it. It has become a timeless classic. Christmas wouldn't be the same without Wallace and Gromit.

Opposite: Wallace and Gromit pose for the camera. Overleaf: Early sketches from Nick Park.

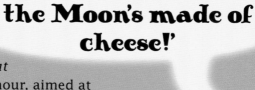

'Everybody knows the Moon's made of cheese!'

Plot

Wallace is sitting in his front room, carefully reading through holiday brochures. He and Gromit need a break from their usual routine, but he can't think of anywhere to go. Skiing doesn't really appeal, but that seems to be all he can find in the brochures.

Deciding that he should take a break from the hunt for a nice holiday, Wallace potters into the kitchen to make himself a nice plate of cheese and crackers. The cupboard is full of packets of crackers, all right, but the fridge is woefully bereft of cheese. They've run out!

Wallace rushes back to the front room and pulls out the last brochure – *Cheese Holidays* – but to no avail. There's nothing available quickly that will satisfy his craving. Turning, he gazes longingly out of the window at the distant Moon. 'Everybody knows the Moon's made of cheese!' he tells an uncertain Gromit. It'll mean a bit of heavy engineering, but Wallace has never been averse to inventing something when it's the only way to get what he wants. He'll build a rocket!

COUNT DOWN 54

INT. CELLAR. ROCKET.   'A GRAND DAY OUT'.   NICK PARK.

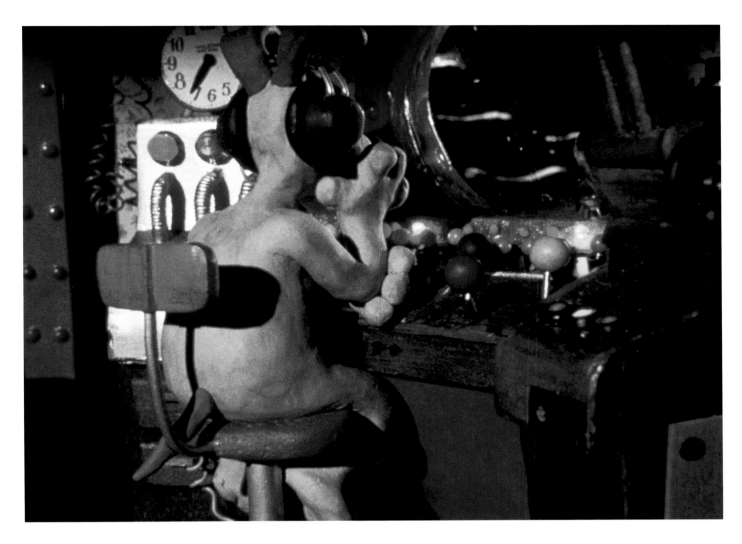

Actor Peter Hawkins provided a voice for Gromit (he also, bizarrely, provided voices for the Daleks and the Cybermen in Doctor Who), but Nick eventually decided to drop the idea of Gromit speaking when it became clear how expressive the dog could be just through small movements of his eyes and brow. The voice was never heard.

Down in the cellar, Wallace starts putting together his plans. After a few false starts when his blueprints quickly mutate into games of noughts and crosses, he manages to design the perfect rocket ship – one powerful enough to take a man and his dog to the Moon in search of cheese. And bring them back again.

Construction proceeds quickly, despite the occasional accident (such as the bit of Gromit's drill getting stuck in a plank of wood, sending him spinning rapidly around). Within what seems like only a few moments, the spacecraft is complete – a bright orange behemoth liberally held together with rivets.

In contrast to the Northern Industrial design of the rocket's outside, the interior is nicely furnished. and wallpapered to boot. Gromit settles himself down in front of a control console with headphones on and waits for Wallace.

Outside, Wallace uses a match to light the all-important fuse. As he clambers into the rocket, a hatch high above slides to one side, revealing the hole in the vegetable patch through which the rocket will emerge.

The fuse is burning steadily down now, but Wallace makes an unhappy discovery. In all the kerfuffle of building and launching the

rocket, they've lost sight of the purpose of their trip. They've forgotten to pack any crackers for their lunar picnic! Quickly, while the burning fuse gets shorter and shorter, Wallace scrambles down the ladder affixed to the side of the ship, up the cellar stairs and into the kitchen. Weighed down by boxes of crackers he stumbles back down into the cellar, up the ladder and into the rocket, slamming the heavy door shut just as the flame on the fuse reaches the rocket.

Nothing happens.

Shamefacedly, Gromit reaches down and releases the hand-brake. The rocket leaps into the air, blasting its way through the atmosphere and forcing the mice in the cellar to put on sunglasses to protect their eyes from the glare.

The trip to the Moon is long enough that Wallace and Gromit have to pass the time somehow. Gromit practises his card-sharping skills, while Wallace reads the *Evening Post* (headline: 'Chicken Saved by Bantam').

Eventually, they reach the Moon. The rocket lands safely, and the two picnickers emerge on the surface, looking around in wonder, amazement and hunger. Contrary to scientific reports, the Moon's surface is yellow, great spires reach up toward the heavens in the distance and there's a breathable atmosphere.

Wallace and Gromit sit down and set out their picnic accoutrements. Wallace uses a kitchen knife to carve a hunk of cheese from the Moon's surface. Gingerly, he eats it. It's nice, but he can't quite place the taste.

After a few rounds of cheese and crackers, Wallace and Gromit decide to go exploring. Or, rather, Wallace decides to go exploring and Gromit is dragged

Above: The rocket ship heads toward the moon. Opposite: How different would television history have been if Nick Park's character designs had remained as they originally were?

The World of Wallace & Gromit

along. Unfortunately, the Moon's surface is pretty boring, and there's not an awful lot for the two of them to see. The only thing to lighten the tedium is their discovery of a strange mechanical device, like a gas cooker on wheels, with a coin slot in its middle and a wonky antenna. Intrigued, Wallace puts a coin in the slot, but nothing happens. The two of them walk away.

Behind them, the coin has operated a delayed mechanism within the mechanical device. The coin falls, operating a clockwork meter which powers the device. Arms emerge from its sides. It straightens its antenna self-consciously. Retrieving a telescope from a drawer, it scans the horizon for signs of life and is disturbed to find what appears to be a picnic site where someone has been slicing chunks out of the surface and eating them!

The device carefully packs away its telescope and wheels across to the picnic site. After first replacing as much cheese as possible, it then discovers a holiday brochure that Wallace bought with him. Momentarily captivated by the idea of skiing, the device is rudely bought back down to Earth (well, the Moon) when it catches sight of a large, orange rocket dripping oil onto the Moon's pristine surface. Wheeling over to the rocket, the mechanical device writes a warning note and places the note on the rocket's skin. It obviously objects to people carving chunks out of the Moon and dripping oil all over it.

'No crackers, Gromit! We've forgotten the crackers!'

Gazing around for the owners of the rocket, the device catches sight of Wallace and Gromit in the distance. It speeds towards them, removing what looks like a large club from its drawer, but just as it is about to hit Wallace over the head, Wallace's ten pence runs out. The device freezes in mid-gesture – much to Gromit's incredulity. Wallace, oblivious, decides it's time to pack up and go, but before he does – and before Gromit can stop him – he absent-mindedly puts another ten pence in the coin slot on the front of the device.

Moments later, the device comes back to life. Confused by the fact that the victim of its attack has suddenly vanished, it takes a few moments to gather its thoughts. Suddenly it notices that the two trespassers are about to leave in their rocket – and with them go possibly its only chance to find out what skiing really feels like. Desperate, it rushes towards the rocket.

On board the rocket, Wallace and Gromit suddenly realize that what appears to be a lunatic robotic denizen of the lunar surface is heading for them at a fair lick, with what they assume is the intention of stopping them from taking

Above: The cooker scans the horizon for signs of life. Overleaf: Nick's original sketches for the cooker, including articulated hands.

The World of Wallace & Gromit

off. They lock the door and pray that the robot can't get in, but they've forgotten to light the fuse!

Outside, the robotic device pulls a tin opener from its drawer and starts attacking the ship. It manages to create a hole large enough to climb through, but breaks a pipe in the process. Taking out a match so it can see what it is doing in the darkened interior of the ship, it accidentally sets light to the fuel gushing from the broken pipe, blasting the rocket into orbit but accidentally falling back out of the hole as it does so. Lying abandoned on the lunar surface, the robot watches forlornly as the rocket carrying Wallace and Gromit recedes into the distance. Its spirits perk up as it realizes that some of the detritus that fell from the rocket as it launched resembles the skis that it saw on the cover of the interlopers' holiday brochure. Experimentally, it picks up one of the pieces of metal and bends it. This might just work! And even before Wallace and Gromit's rocket has vanished from the sky, the robotic device is skiing up and down the cheesy spires of the Moon, using two bent pieces of metal as skis.

> 'Daylight robbery. They always nick your money, them flipping machines...'

Behind the scenes

It's somehow comforting to discover that Nick Park approached the making of the first Wallace and Gromit film in the same spirit of painstaking attention to detail, and obliviousness to time, as Wallace himself does when constructing one of his inventions. The story behind *A Grand Day Out* began when Nick was a student at the National Film and Television School.

'In my degree course at Sheffield,' Nick explains, 'I had experimented with drawn animation and a bit of plasticine, but mainly I worked with puppet animation. It was all influenced by *Noggin the Nog* and *The Clangers*, but then when I went to Film School, I didn't know what technique to use. I was interested in children's book illustration: I had been writing a couple of little stories that weren't really going anywhere, and they had a couple of characters, just sketches really, of a cat and a bloke.'

The cat would later transmute into a dog, of course, and the man would lose the moustache that Nick had originally drawn him with, but the genesis of the ingenious inventor and the cautious canine was there, in Nick Park's student sketchbook.

'Later on,' Nick continues, 'I did a three week attachment at Elstree Film Studios, making tea for the special effects unit on Jim Henson and Frank Oz's film *The Dark Crystal* and seeing how they were doing the special effects. I was learning a lot, and I was starting to piece together this idea which started with this guy who builds a rocket in his basement. I went back to these kids' book illustrations that I had done, and took these characters and thought, yeah, it could be really simple. A man and his dog! I called them Wallace and Gromit, and that's how it started. They build a rocket in his basement and want to go to the Moon. Why would he want to go to the Moon? Maybe it's made of cheese. It was as simple as that.'

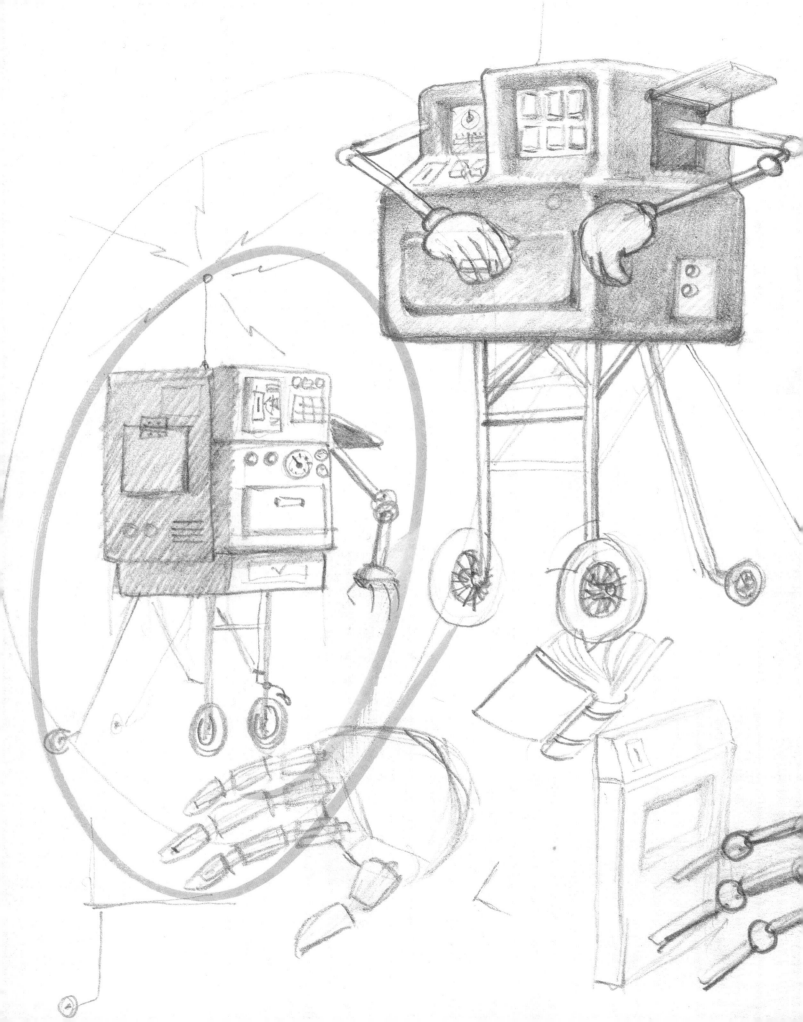

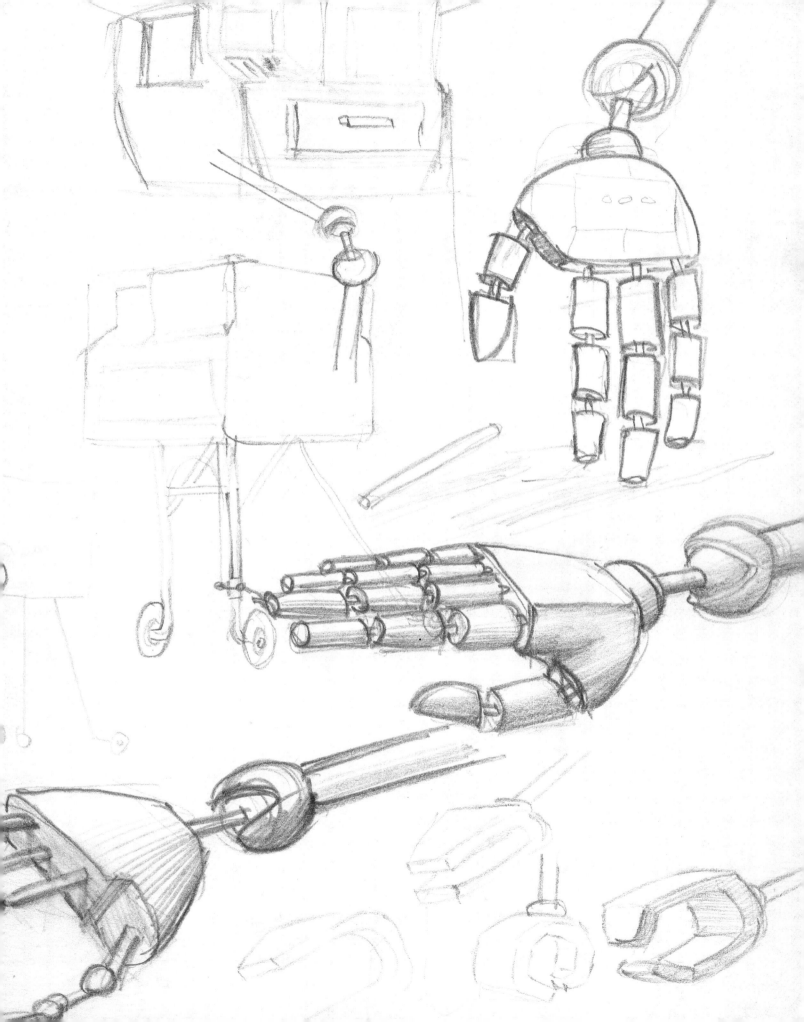

The idea and the sketches were a start, of course, but in order to convert them to reality Nick needed something more formal to work from. Something like a script.

'The very first script, I worked on with a friend I shared digs with in Sheffield called Steve Rushton. He was into writing kids books. He was a painter. We sat down in a pub and wrote it. He did the typing really. It started off from that script.'

That's where it started, and that's where it might have ended as well if it hadn't been for a fortuitous meeting between two creative geniuses.

'What happened,' recalls David Sproxton, co-founder (with Peter Lord) of Aardman Animations, 'was that we went up to give a talk about animation to the National Film School. We thought, "This is stupid, we haven't had any formal training ourselves – talk about the blind leading the blind!"'

During David Sproxton and Peter Lord's visit, Nick Park took the opportunity to show them what he was making for his final year project – a short animated film about a Northern inventor and his dog.

'I remember,' says David Sproxton, 'he was doing the cellar set: the construction of the rocket sequence. He hadn't actually shot much more than that. There was probably some dialogue with Peter Sallis doing the voice. But as to how the film was going to pan out, we had no idea because we simply didn't have time to look at the storyboards on that day.'

'I thought it would be a ten-minute film, and it would take me six months to make,' Nick admits. 'I didn't think it would be a lifetime journey. Even then, I had no idea that the film would take me six or seven years to make. In fact, I remember the script for *A Grand Day Out* was about 20 pages long, and on about page 3 it says, "There now follows a sequence where Wallace and Gromit build a rocket." It was just a paragraph. I started on that paragraph, and a year and a half later, I actually finished the sequence!'

There was, however, enough in existence to impress the two professional animators, and to give them a reason to remember Nick.

'Certainly when we met him at the film school,' David recalls, 'there was something about what he was trying to do which was actually a bit different. You could immediately see that. It was an ambitious project: there was something about the way he was using the plasticine and the sets and things that he'd built which was actually very charming, but it also showed a real endeavour which you didn't often see. So we definitely kept in touch with him for two or three years.'

What became clear to David and Peter was that Nick had actually bitten off more than he could chew.

'We realized that his film was never really going to get finished in the way in which he was making it. The Film School was a slightly self-service environment in those days. Nick had a very small studio in which to shoot the thing, and because he worked in a solitary way he was having to do everything himself. In those days it was a three-year course, but you didn't graduate until you had completed your final

Opposite: Wallace attempts to identify the cheese he's found on the moon.

'Plate, knife, cracker ...'

The World of Wallace & Gromit

'Ooh, it's different . . .
Camembert?'

year project, or consumed the production budget. The budgets that people were given for their final year project were something like £8,000, which was quite a lot in the mid-eighties. And Nick didn't have anybody to pay. I think Peter Sallis had done it as a favour, so the rest of it went on materials. But at the end of five odd years he'd only made about six or seven minutes. It was a very, very slow process.'

At which point, David had a brainwave.

'We needed somebody to help on a film we were making for Channel Four called *Babylon*,' he recalls. 'I remember saying, "This is getting silly: Nick's never going to finish it, he's a great animator, why doesn't he come and join us and we'll help him finish it once we've got through this other piece?" Which is basically what we did. We said, "Nick, bring your camera down, bring your sets down, we'll give you some space and we'll help support you and our model makers can help finish it." And so he joined us, I think, in 1985.'

By that time, Nick had not only finished the rocket construction sequence, but also completed some other key scenes.

INT. ROCKET. "BREAKER 1 A, BREAKER 1 A, ARE THERE ANY BIG BUDDIES OUT THERE? DO YOU COPY? DO I HAVE ANY EXTRA TERRESTRIAL LIFE FORMS, COME IN?"

'I think he'd done that gag with the sawing, and Gromit on the drill spinning round,' David recalls. 'And the stuff with the noughts and crosses on the drawing board. I think he'd also shot the looking up to the grating part.'

Above: The interior of the rocket.

'I spent a year and a half on Wallace and Gromit,' Nick Park recalls, 'but then my money and time ran out. I was still halfway through the film so they let me carry on. I was quite desperate, because I had no money for quite a long time, and then Aardman offered me some work. So I worked for them over the summer a couple of times to get some money, and then finally they said, "Come to work for us part time," but it would have meant I couldn't finish the film. I didn't want to be an assistant animator for years to come. I had a vision, I wanted to direct. And so, in the end, they said, "Well, work for us part time and we'll help you make your film. We can work it out with the film school." That was perfect. I'd be working on a commercial for two months, and then the film for a month. On and off, it took another four years to complete!'

Nick's attention was to be taken away from Wallace and Gromit for a while, however. Under the terms of the agreement between him and Aardman, he had to help them on their projects first before he could get back to his own one.

'We'd also been commissioned to do five films for Channel 4,' says David, 'of which Nick Park's *Creature*

Comforts became one. And then in spring, 1986 we all went off to New York for three or four months to work on the *Pee-Wee Herman Show*. We came back in the autumn, finished *Babylon* and then literally, within six months, *A Grand Day Out* was finished. Nick worked on it fairly solidly, I did a bit of lighting for him, and it was very quickly wrapped up.'

'Quickly', of course, is a relative term.

'Actually, the whole film was shot over about seven years,' David Sproxton laughs.

'Set co-ordinates for 62 West Wallaby Street!'

Even though Nick took his final year project with him when he went to Aardman, the link back to the National Film and Television School was never quite broken. As they were responsible for funding the start of the film, they also get a cut of the profits under an agreement with Aardman.

'Actually, it's been quite a nice little earner for the Film School over the years,' David Sproxton says. 'And we're very happy, because it has put money back to the grass roots, and it's supplied them with a fair chunk of funding.'

One of the reasons why Nick Park was taking his time over the animation of *A Grand Day Out* was that he had written far too much material for the time and resources he had to hand, but he was too close to the whole thing to be able to make the necessary cuts. It took the presence of David and Peter to persuade him that certain elements just had to go.

'It runs to about 23 minutes now,' David states. 'It probably would have run to pushing 40. The storyboard went on forever.'

One sequence in particular had Wallace and Gromit discover a fast-food restaurant on the Moon. Wonderful though that might have been, David and Peter managed to persuade him that it could be removed without hurting the story.

'Gosh, yes,' Nick recalls now, 'the original story was that Wallace and Gromit were going to go to the Moon, and there were going to be a whole lot of characters there. One of them was a parking meter attendant, which was the only one that remained – the robot cooker character – but there were going to be aliens, and all sorts. There was going to be a McDonalds on the Moon, and it was going to be like a spoof *Star Wars*. Wallace was going to get thrown into prison and Gromit was going to have to get him out. By the time I came to Aardman, I had just started doing the Moon scene and somebody told me, 'It's going to take you another nine years if you do that scene!' so I had to have a check with reality and cut that whole bit out. Somehow I had to tie up the story on the Moon, and finish the film.'

A Grand Day Out was finished, and was transmitted by Channel 4 on Christmas Eve, 1990. And that might have been the end of it, except that somehow the charm and warmth of Nick's creations struck a chord not only with the general public but also with critics and other practitioners of animation. It became a talking point, as did Nick's other project, the short Channel 4 film *Creature Comforts*. Aardman knew that Nick was talented, they knew that his work was somehow special, but nobody there could have predicted that both *A Grand Day Out* and *Creature Comforts* would

A Grand Day Out is the only one of the three original Wallace and Gromit films not to win an Oscar. It lost out to another Nick Park creation – *Creature Comforts*.

be nominated for Academy Awards. When they were, everyone there was stunned.

'I don't think it actually hit us,' David recalls, 'because although we were getting awards for some of the work that we did for Channel Four, we thought, "You've got to be joking, it's ridiculous, we're never going to win an Oscar!" You don't think of it in those terms. And when it did happen, when our nomination came in, it was a huge thing for a British movie to get nominations in this category. It very rarely happened. And certainly to have two in a three-horse race was pretty extraordinary.'

In the end, *Creature Comforts* won the 1990 Academy Award in the Short Film – Animated category, while *A Grand Day Out* had to make do with the not inconsiderable honour of being a nominee, alongside Bruno Bozzetto's *Grasshoppers*. One does have to wonder, however – if it had been Aardman's other film of the time, *Babylon*, that had gained the acclaim and the prizes, and *A Grand Day Out* had sunk without anything more than a slight ripple – what would Nick Park have done? Would it have marked the end of Wallace and Gromit?

'Hold tight, lad, and think of Lancashire hotpot!'

Opposite: Gromit is amazed they've got away in one piece, more or less.
Below: The two pieces they leave behind are put to good use.

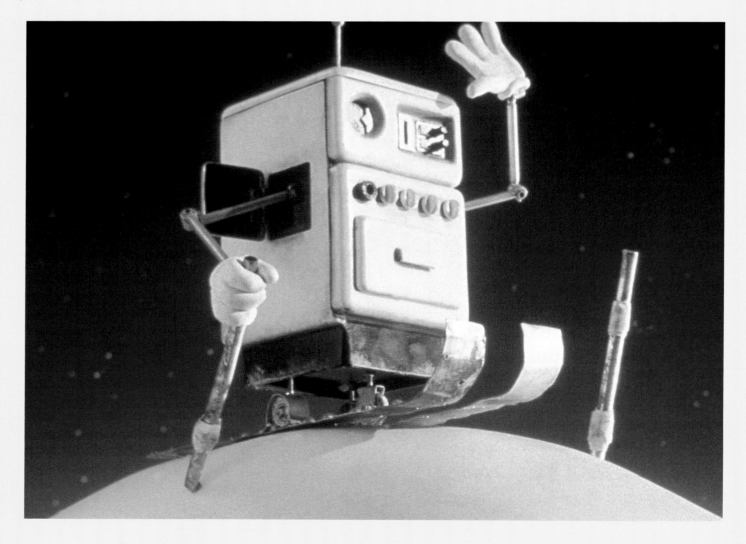

The World of Wallace & Gromit

David Sproxton, for one, is pretty sure that the world would have heard from the idiosyncratic inventor and his canine companion again. 'He's so stubborn, is Nick, and so sure-footed, that I think he would have just carried on. I think he probably would have thought, "Oh, I see, I just need to do some tweaks," I don't think he would have ever thought, "These guys are fundamentally wrong, I need to have a bishop and a cat," or something. Or he might have said, "Gromit's the wrong colour" or "He needs to speak," but I think the idea that fundamentally they're not going to work would not have occurred to him.'

Although he never realized it at the time, Nick Park can look back on *A Grand Day Out* now and see very clearly where the inspiration for Wallace came from.

During the filming of *A Grand Day Out*, in the scene where Gromit is welding the rocket together, a sparkler was used to provide the special effects. The sparkler caused the set to catch fire, melting Gromit's nozzle before it was put out!

'I wasn't really basing Wallace on anybody particularly,' he says, 'but after making the film it became very apparent that he was incredibly like my dad in many ways, particularly because of his whole attitude to life. He's naive – not that my dad was naive, but he had ideas and got on with them. The way the rocket was built like a little living room in space, with wallpaper and all these practical domestic appliances, I suddenly realized that was my dad. Particularly as, when I was a kid, he had bought this old caravan, and scrapped it and did it up again. Inside it was like a living room with wallpaper and chairs and everything in it. The whole family went on holiday in this caravan. It was uncanny, it was so close to the film!'

'There goes my knotted pine'
The Wrong Trousers

Channel 4 had transmitted *A Grand Day Out*, but it was the BBC who commissioned its sequel – *The Wrong Trousers*. It showed both of them on Christmas Day and Boxing Day, 1993, respectively – a television event. *The Wrong Trousers* was an altogether more accomplished piece of work: the plot is sharper, the script wittier, the style even more cinematic, the animation more lovingly detailed, and yet the same essential humour and characterization shine through. It also takes place in the same recognizably offbeat world, one where a penguin can just wander in off the street and take up residence without anyone batting an eyelid.

The Wrong Trousers has been described as the greatest thirty minutes of animation ever made, and there aren't that many people who would disagree. Nick Park's animation (aided by colleague Steve Box) is a major reason behind that, but the clever script (co-written by Nick and *Doctor Who* scribe Bob Baker) also plays a large part. The genius of the script lies in its sheer unpredictability; once you get to the end, everything that happens makes sense, but there's no way of predicting from the beginning what's going to happen. The clever structure was driven by the need to connect together a whole series of isolated sketches by Nick Park, but whatever the reason, it works beautifully.

Above top: Gromit fetches the morning paper, just like a normal dog.
Above: Gromit's birthday card. No expense spared.
Opposite: Wallace demonstrates his newly acquired techno-trousers to a surprised Gromit.

Plot

It's Gromit's birthday. Keen to find out what surprises the day has in store for him – and what presents Wallace might have bought – Gromit is having a quiet cup of tea and some toast in the kitchen (which, for reasons more to do with Wallace's eccentric interests than with anything logical, has a set of miniature train tracks snaking around it and out through the door). Upstairs, Wallace is fast asleep in bed.

The post arrives, clattering onto the front door mat. Gromit rushes from the kitchen to see what's arrived. Birthday cards perhaps? Maybe even some

'They're techno-trousers.
Ex-NASA. Fantastic
for walkies.'

Gromit's birthday is 12th February, and in *The Wrong Trousers* he eagerly marks this date on the calendar. Every year there is a birthday greeting posted for Gromit in *The Daily Telegraph*.

presents? Unfortunately, the doughty dog is doomed to be disappointed – it's all for Wallace.

Meanwhile, the noise of the postman has woken up Wallace. Stretching, he rings a bell to alert Gromit to the beginning of their normal 'rise and shine' routine.

Down in the kitchen again, Gromit pulls a lever, setting in motion one of Wallace's latest inventions – the combined Dressotron and Breakfast Dispenser.

Upstairs, Wallace's bed tips up to an almost vertical position. Expecting this, Wallace confidently slides out through the bottom of the bed and plummets through a trapdoor that has opened up in the floor of his room. Smiling benignly, he falls through a waiting pair of trousers, held aloft by robot arms that have emerged from the walls of the kitchen and into an empty chair at the end of the kitchen table. Another set of automated arms pull on his shirt sleeves for him, then a small robotic device scoots up behind and pulls his tank top over his head (with shirt collar and tie already attached). As a final

Above: Wallace uses his model railway to deliver a present to Gromit over breakfast.

touch, a spring-loaded device splats jam at his face: jam which is intercepted by toast jumping out from the toaster and landing perfectly on his plate.

Wallace's invention appears to be working perfectly, which isn't what Gromit would normally have expected.

Dressed and breakfasted, Wallace cheerily opens the post, but they're all bills! Concerned at their dwindling cash reserves, he comes to a momentous decision. He's going to let the spare room out to a lodger!

With a merry *toot!* a miniature train trundles into the kitchen, controlled by Wallace. It's got a present on it – a present for Gromit! Eagerly, the dog tears open the wrapping paper, but the clever canine is crushed. It's a collar and lead. Gromit is not impressed.

Wallace cheerfully tells Gromit that there are more presents to come. Gromit is momentarily cheered up – but only momentarily. Wallace's idea of more presents is a pair of robotic legs swathed in wrapping paper. Ignoring Gromit's disappointed gaze, Wallace proudly tells him that they are techno-trousers – originally developed by NASA but now perfect for taking Gromit for walkies. Keen to demonstrate, Wallace ties Gromit's new collar to the techno-trousers and fiddles with the controls. The techno-trousers set off, striding out of the house and pulling Gromit after them.

Once they are out of Wallace's sight, Gromit replaces himself with a toy dog on wheels. Oblivious, the trousers go off by

'You look like somebody owns you, now.'

The World of Wallace & Gromit

Above: Gromit is singularly unimpressed with his hand-made birthday card.

themselves through the park while Gromit plays in the children's playground.

When Gromit returns from walkies – sitting on the wheeled toy dog platform and letting the techno-trousers pull him along – Wallace has put a sign in the window alerting passers by to the fact that they have a room to let.

Within moments, it seems, a visitor arrives to see the spare room – a penguin with small, beady eyes. He stares balefully at Gromit. Gromit stares back. There's going to be trouble there, the dog can just sense it.

Wallace takes the penguin upstairs to see the spare room, talking all the while, but the penguin has other ideas. Unimpressed with the peeling wallpaper and the pictures falling off the walls, he immediately moves into Gromit's room instead. Wallace is slightly taken aback, but decides to avoid a direct confrontation.

Gromit, disgruntled, moves into the spare room, but at least Wallace helps him redecorate. Gromit uses the techno-trousers to walk up the walls and paint the ceiling whilst Wallace applies wallpaper. Pretty soon, the room is looking spiffing. Life would be rosy, if only the Penguin didn't have a fondness for playing organ music late into the night. (He's especially fond of 'Tie A Yellow Ribbon'.) The noise forces Gromit to sleep out in the backyard – and he's surprised when, late one night, the penguin comes in through the garden gate when Gromit thought he was in his room.

Wallace's inventions in *The Wrong Trousers* perhaps owe a debt not only to the drawings of English artist Heath Robinson but also Snub Pollard's classic 1923 comedy *It's a Gift*, which includes, at least in spirit if not in actual detail, many of the devices Wallace builds for waking up and having his breakfast.

'Nice drop of Bordeaux this, eh?'

Opposite: The penguin
makes himself comfortable
in Gromit's room. The
penguin's presence is
deeply disturbing for
Gromit, who believes that
his place by Wallace's side
is being usurped.

**'Oh, dear me.
We shall have to economise,
Gromit.'**

It doesn't take long for the penguin to usurp Gromit's place in the West Wallaby Street household. Not only does he redecorate Gromit's room – replacing Gromit's nice bone-pattern wallpaper with a fish-pattern design – but he also becomes Wallace's trusted helper – putting Wallace's slippers on him before Gromit can get to them, and taking him the morning paper. Gromit feels more and more isolated. He has no place in the house any more. And so he decides to leave. Packing up his few remaining possessions, he hits the road. In Gromit's room, the penguin is reading a book on electronics. He picks up a drill and operates it in an experimental manner. He has a plan, and it's not one that either Wallace or Gromit would approve of.

Next morning, Wallace wakes up at his usual time and stretches. Time for breakfast and a leisurely read of the paper before settling down to some serious inventing. But before he can ring for breakfast his bed tips up and he slides down through the trapdoor in his bedroom floor, heading for the kitchen. This is a little premature, but he's shocked when he falls into not his own comfortable trousers but the ex-NASA techno-trousers! Worse, the controls have been removed! He can't stop them! Concerned, he calls for Gromit, but there's no response. As the techno-trousers start walking out of the house and down the street, Wallace begins dimly to realize that he's on his own.

Out in the town, Gromit has spent an uncomfortable night sleeping in a dustbin. Realizing he can't go on like that for much longer, he scours the windows of tobacconists' shops for accommodation. He doesn't find anything suitable – but he does find himself strangely intrigued by a 'Wanted' poster for a criminal chicken. There's something about the picture of the chicken that reminds him of the penguin that has usurped his place in Wallace's affections.

While Gromit is gazing into the tobacconist's shop window, Wallace rushes past, still wearing the techno-trousers. He yells something about the trousers having gone haywire, but before Gromit can leap to Wallace's aid he catches sight of the penguin with the remote control unit. And he's not attempting to stop the trousers from running off with Wallace; instead, he appears to be actively controlling them. Gromit decides to bide his time, and follows the penguin through the town. They eventually end up at the local museum where the penguin is absorbed in making notes, drawing sketches and measuring windows. Gromit is intrigued and concerned.

Above: A depressed Gromit packs his few possessions and leaves 62 West Wallaby Street.

Later that night, the techno-trousers bring Wallace home. He falls into bed, exhausted, and is asleep within moments – still wearing the trousers.

Once everything is dark and quiet, Gromit sneaks back into the house – through what used to be the dog-flap, but is now the penguin-flap. On the table in what used to be Gromit's room, but is now the penguin's room, are detailed plans of the town's museum and its latest exhibit – the Blue Diamond!

Suddenly, Gromit hears the penguin-flap flapping. The penguin is back in the house! Quickly, the dog rushes into Wallace's room and hides under the bedsheets. Moments later the penguin walks past the door to the room, wearing what looks like a fake rubber comb on the top of his head to make him look like a chicken. Shocked, Gromit remembers the 'Wanted' poster in the tobacconist's window. Can it be true? Is their lodger really the wanted criminal known as 'Feathers' McGraw?

The penguin operates the remote control for the techno-trousers, and Wallace – still asleep, and wearing a rather bizarre crash helmet – strides out of the house and down the street. Meanwhile, Gromit has become caught up in the Dressotron and Breakfast Dispenser, which appears to have become accidentally engaged. Before he even knows what's going on he's been flipped downstairs into Wallace's real trousers and hit in the face with a dollop of jam.

For the rain effect in *The Wrong Trousers* little blobs of glycerine were put onto glass and animated by being blown, frame by frame, down the transparent surface.

The World of Wallace & Gromit

'It's the wrong trousers, Gromit, and they've gone wrong!'

A scene written in the script but never actually filmed would have explained the origin of the techno-trousers. *The Wrong Trousers* was meant to start with an astronaut undertaking a spacewalk while wearing them, only to lose them and watch as they plummeted toward the Earth.

Out in the town, the penguin gets the sleeping Wallace to walk up the wall of the museum while standing on his chest. Together, the diminutive Arctic bird and the sleeping inventor keep going until they get to the roof. Without stopping, Wallace walks (or is walked) up the side of ventilator shaft and then, attached by the magnetic boots, down its massive throat and into the bowels of the building. The ventilation system eventually disgorges Wallace into the room where the Blue Diamond is being exhibited, and the penguin carefully guides him across the ceiling, upside down, above the laser beams and other security systems, eventually stopping him directly above the impressive diamond. Fiddling with the remote controls, the penguin demonstrates another invention – a small crane that emerges from Wallace's crash helmet which is lowered in order to retrieve the diamond from its display case.

Suddenly, a ceiling tile gives way! One foot of the techno-trousers swings loose, and Wallace's crash-helmeted head passes through a laser beam. Alarms go off and shutters start coming down over all the windows. Panicking, the penguin guides Wallace out through the nearest window, with the diamond, before the shutter can come fully down, but the commotion wakes up Wallace.

'Feathers' McGraw rushes Wallace, the diamond and the techno-trousers back to West Wallaby Street and locks Wallace in cupboard. He is about to make off with his ill-gotten loot when he is confronted by a vengeful Gromit with a rolling pin! Sadly for Gromit, the penguin has a gun. He locks Gromit in the wardrobe with Wallace.

Frantically, Gromit rewires the techno-trousers in order to get them working independently of the penguin's remote-control unit. Successful,

Many members of Aardman's technical construction team, which is responsible for constructing everything used behind the camera lens, from brackets to motors, used to work for British Aerospace in the Bristol area. Some of them were actually involved in building Concorde.

Above left: The evil penguin tries out the remote control for the techno-trousers. Above right: Laser beams criss-cross the museum whilst a sleeping Wallace is suspended from the ceiling. Opposite top: Wallace 'drops off' while walking up the museum wall. Opposite bottom: 'Feathers' McGraw admires his superb chicken disguise.

he uses them to batter through the wardrobe and sets off in pursuit of the thief.

'Feathers' McGraw slides down the banister and lands on Wallace's toy train. A chase ensues, with the penguin at the front of train, Gromit in the middle and Wallace balancing on one foot, still wearing the techno-trousers, at the end. Wallace ends up on a parallel line; Gromit frantically has to lay more pieces of track when he starts running out, and the entire thing eventually ends in a massive crash, during which the penguin flies through the air and is caught by a triumphant Gromit in a milk bottle. The thief is finally taken away in custody and Wallace and Gromit settle down in comfort, their financial security assured by the reward money for his capture.

Behind the scenes

Following the wild success of *A Grand Day Out*, it was obvious to everyone at Aardman that Wallace and Gromit's adventures were only just beginning. The question was, however, what form those adventures should take.

'I had great aspirations for the characters in *A Grand Day Out*,' Nick Park recalls, 'and a lot of that was realized, but I always had more in mind for them, and I felt that I was just starting to learn my craft, if you like. There's a lot about the story that's very linear and naive. I set out without a real story in mind, to be honest. Once I started at Aardman and got more experience with commercials, and thought more about short films, I realized that I wanted something that stretched me, something with more storytelling, plot and structure.'

The road that would lead to the next short film – *The Wrong Trousers* – was, however, not particularly well mapped out. In fact, it was a mass of loose ends.

'Nick had got a lot of ideas for *The Wrong Trousers*,' David Sproxton recalls. 'His sketchbook was full of stuff – a whole bundle of ideas – but there was no story there.'

'Well, this is a fine how-do-you-do, isn't it Gromit?'

Many of the ideas in Nick's sketchbook would later turn up in the finished film, but at the time Nick had no plot to connect them together. 'I had in my sketchbooks all these basic ideas about a penguin coming to stay,' he says. 'I'd had the idea for years, since the beginning of *A Grand Day Out*. I also had the idea of the techno-trousers – these space trousers that you wear – becoming remote controlled.'

'Well,' David Sproxton says, 'in his sketchbook you will see a whole train chase sequence storyboarded out, apropos of nothing at all. And there's this penguin. I think there's possibly even a picture of a penguin with a rubber glove on its head. And what's interesting is that in his sketchbook, sort of randomly scattered over a year or two, were some of the key images that went into *The Wrong Trousers*, but Nick couldn't find a way of making them all join up.'

'I tried writing it a bit with Pete [Lord], but we didn't really get very far,' Nick admits. 'I tried with another chap called Brian Sibley, who'd written books on *Chicken Run* and adapted *The Lord of the Rings* for radio back in the eighties. We made some progression there, but that didn't work out. Then I found Bob Baker, a writer in Bristol, who had a lot of experience and was able to give me a lot of good sound advice. He helped shape up the story into a plot that really worked.'

Aardman were already in intermittent contact with Bob Baker through some work they had been doing for HTV.

'I knew the Aardman people from when they began,' Bob Baker explains. 'I was always in live action: I'd followed their work from the beginning, from the very first Morph days before Nick Park joined them. I used to go down and see them in their studio and everything. Colin Rose at the BBC knew me, they knew me, and Colin said, "Well, how about Bob Baker?" So there was this very strange meeting. They were all watching Nick and me talking … and we got on very well!'

The process of writing the script wasn't quite what Bob Baker was expecting, however.

Above left: Gromit bravely confronts the evil penguin with a rolling pin.
Above right: 'Feathers' McGraw turns the tables and locks the fearless investigators in the wardrobe.
Opposite: Nick Park's sketches for The Wrong Trousers, *and an evil genius.*

'Well, that went as well as could be expected, didn't it?'

The building in which *The Wrong Trousers* was filmed used to be an old banana-ripening shed. Aardman still have offices there to this day.

The World of Wallace & Gromit

'To begin with,' he recalls, 'Nick showed me his thoughts on another half-hour, and there were, like, two hundred ideas: wild, mad, crazy ideas. And I said, "Well, let's pick some out – which ones do we want to do? What kind of story is it?'

'That's where Bob's skill was,' David Sproxton recalls. 'He could lay them all out and say, "Oh, I've got it – here's the story!" He basically sewed the whole thing together to make what became a very credible story, using these key images. And it's staggering, actually, because he literally looked through the sketchbook, saw this set of images which were completely disconnected and then said "Da-da!" Bob became a kind of catalyst, a bit like a ... almost like a scribe, he structured the stuff, but he could bring out an awful lot of the comedy that was in Nick's head really, really well.'

One of the sketches Nick Park showed Bob was of the penguin with beady eyes and a simple bottle-shaped body. Both of them felt there was something there they could use.

'First he was a character in a zoo,' says Bob, 'and then he was something else, so I said, "Why don't we make him into a baddie because he's a nice, sinister character?"'

Having decided that the penguin was going to be the villain of the piece, that gave Nick Park and Bob Baker the beginnings of a structure. If there was a villain, for instance, there had to be a crime ...

'Simple story: a robbery,' Bob says. 'And keeping to those very simple things, with the humanity of the Wallace and Gromit characters and the very specific way that they react with each other, it just made it perfect, somehow. It just seemed to work!'

Above and below: The exciting train chase in The Wrong Trousers.

'Most definitely not legal, this.'

The World of Wallace & Gromit

Surprisingly, given that Nick and Bob had to winnow their way through so many initial ideas before they could connect the ones they had into a coherent plot, the actual process didn't take particularly long.

'Oh, I think it was about three months,' Bob recalls. 'The hard work you do in the very beginning. The working out of the outline, that's the hard work. Getting it into a state where you can say to somebody, "There it is, that's what it's about!" That is your blueprint: you work on that from there on, and actually writing the script is like going downhill because you've done the hard work.'

As many people have found, one of the main causes of delay is trying to get together with the phenomenally busy Nick Park.

'We only worked on the script when we came together,' Bob remembers, 'but he was so busy that I didn't see him. "Nick can spare an hour on Thursday!" – that sort of thing. We did the odd half day and full day together, but if you put the days together in total it wasn't that many.'

'I'll give you what for, you tyke!'

The train chase was filmed with the camera and the train both attached to a central rig which was free to move along a 20 foot long track. The entire rig was pushed along and the camera shutter opened for two seconds (or ten centimetres of movement). This was enough to blur the background whilst keeping the train and characters rock steady.

Given the difficulty of getting the two writers in the same room at the same time, one might have expected the script to have come out short. In fact, early drafts were far too long!

'I think at one point *The Wrong Trousers* was something like 70 or 80 pages long!' Bob recalls. 'We had to cut right back to about 40 pages. We were going hammer and tongs at cutting it.'

Unlike *A Grand Day Out*, where an entire sequence set in a lunar fast-food restaurant was cut out, the material removed from *The Wrong Trousers* by Nick and Bob was minor stuff that didn't contribute to the overall thrust of the plot.

'Little things,' Bob remembers, 'not whole sequences. Things like where Wallace or Gromit would go off to do something which wasn't relevant to that particular part of the plot. So you say, "Well, that's fun, but it ain't relevant."'

Once the script and storyboards were finalized, filming could start. Whereas *A Grand Day Out* was almost entirely Nick Park's work from beginning to end, the production schedule on *The Wrong Trousers* meant that Nick would have to work with someone else. The animator he chose was Steve Box, who had come to Aardman fresh from working for another Bristol animation company on a kids' series called *The Trap Door*. Bizarrely, during his time working on *Trap Door*, Steve had been watching Nick's progress on *A Grand Day Out* with some interest.

As Steve remembers: 'Our editor at the time, Rob Copeland, was editing *A Grand Day Out* as a favour to Nick. He would often bring it in and work on our Steinbeck editing machine, so I would watch it in the making. At the time, I thought what I was seeing was a little bit childish. *Trapdoor* to us was so crazy and colourful. We thought this middle-aged man and his dog going to the Moon to get cheese was a little bit corny, but we were only seeing odd bits of rushes now and again with no sound. I remember seeing the final thing and thinking how wrong I was, and what a lovely feel it had. It was also interesting, because there were ideas in *A Grand Day Out* that we were having at the same time. We had an idea for a film with robot trousers – we called them "space pants" – which must have been about the same time that Nick was thinking about *The Wrong Trousers*.'

Having moved to Aardman, Steve had begun by working on commercials and health information films, but he wanted to move on to bigger and better things. He didn't realize, however, quite what was in store.

'I'll never forget the day Nick asked me to do it,' he sighs. 'I knew he was storyboarding it, and I remember Nick and I going out of the building to the car park and he said to me, "See you tomorrow, Animator Number 2," and he got in his car and went. I didn't know what he meant. The next day, Chris Moll, who produced *The Wrong Trousers*, said, "Nick wonders if you'd like to be Unit 2?" I had to think long and carefully, and three seconds later I said, "Yes!"'

Above: Steve Box.
Opposite: Storyboards for the first sequence Steve filmed for The Wrong Trousers.

Julian Nott's music for *The Wrong Trousers* was influenced by, amongst other things, Bernard Herrmann, who wrote music for many Alfred Hitchcock movies including, most memorably, *Psycho* (1960).

The World of Wallace & Gromit

  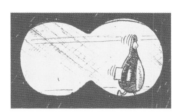 

'At that time, at Aardman,' Steve Box points out, 'it was very much an *auteur* system. There was one person and they would have the idea for their film, and do just about everything. They'd probably have a lighting cameraman, but other than that they would pretty much do the whole thing themselves. It was quite a new thing to have an assistant, and I know Nick says he didn't really know what I was like, so I'm sure he felt nervous letting someone else handle his characters. Basically, the idea was that Nick would take care of Wallace and Gromit, and I would deal mainly with the penguin. It was a simpler character without lip synch, etc.'

Fortunately, it was clear right from the start that bringing Steve in had been the right decision.

'I remember,' he says, 'I did the very first shot: the penguin arriving on a window ledge, and measuring the museum window, sizing up the job with his tape measure. It's quite a long shot – about eleven seconds – and he jumps off again. It came back in rushes, and we were all of us just amazed. The lighting was beautiful, the animation worked well, the tape measure really impressed everybody with the way it moved … We all gathered around the Steinbeck, and we had a feeling that something great was about to happen. I think Nick thought, "Oh, if he can do it that good, I'd better go up a level!" The whole film was incredibly competitive but in a really great way. I was trying to do my best work, and Nick was probably trying to better it,

and the whole level of the animation just jumped up a whole bracket. The same thing happened with Dave Riddett who was Director of Photography, and Tristan Oliver, who was lighting it. The lighting just got better and better. It was gorgeously lit. Some of the backgrounds and sunsets are absolutely superb.'

Steve Box's particular responsibility was the evil penguin, 'Feathers' McGraw. The penguin rapidly became a memorable character in its own right. Small, deliberate and with a very distinctive walk, the evil avian shows absolutely no emotion as it sets about dominating Wallace's household.

'Nick gave Steve Box the task of developing the character in terms of how it would perform, and how it would express itself,' David Sproxton explains. 'He had quite a few weeks to do this, and he realized the less it did, the more menacing it was. So there were the very simple eyes, which don't even move, it only does one walk, which is very determined, and it stops dead. It's very, very disciplined, almost an automaton really. Actually, Steve could have done a lot more with its flippers and could have had it walk in a different way, but the less you do with it the more evil it is. Quite fantastic. I mean there is this bit of plasticine marching about with two black pins for eyes and it's the devil incarnate.'

'He was quite a challenge,' Steve recalls, 'because he had no features, but that was also the thing that gave him the menace and the magic. You were trying to fathom out what he was thinking, and my only tool was being able to move the body shape. I spent a long, long time trying to get his walk right. I've often heard animators say that once the walk is cracked, you've got the character. With the penguin, he had no knees, he just had straight legs, but I desperately wanted him not to bob up and down in a comical way. He had to glide as much as possible, which is very difficult if you haven't got any knees!

'You'll be hearing from my solicitor about this!'

Above: The techno-trousers stagger off into a beautiful sunset.
Opposite: Nick Park at work on The Wrong Trousers. *Note the particularly high-tech way of generating the shadow of a tree on the wall of Wallace's house.*

The World of Wallace & Gromit

The camera used by the animators in *The Wrong Trousers* was originally an old RAF reconnaissance camera, and dated from before World War II. It used to run on clockwork, but was modified by the technical team at Aardman so that it was operated by an electrical motor.

When you step, your legs go apart, so you go lower. The whole thing was a juggle to keep him subtle and thoughtful.'

Although the lack of features was the key to the menace of 'Feathers' McGraw, it did cause Steve some problems in the animation.

'There's only one bit where he shows a lot of clear character,' he says, 'which is when he thinks there's something in the box in the alleyway, and Gromit is hiding inside looking at him through the holes. The penguin stops, and there's a moment where he doesn't move at all. It works really well, because you think, "Oh no, he's seen Gromit!" Then he had to go forward slowly, which should be fairly easy because it should be slow and menacing, but then he had to show that he thought it was nothing. It was very hard, with no expression, no eyebrows and no mouth, to get that feeling of him thinking it was nothing, and moving on. It's all to do with the speed of the movements.'

Although the original idea was that there would be a fairly strict work-share between Nick Park doing Wallace and Gromit, and Steve Box doing 'Feathers' McGraw, things didn't quite work out that way in the end, as Steve explains.

'What happened in *The Wrong Trousers* was that I was supposed to stick to the penguin, but because lip-synch is very time-consuming I would often go through my schedule a lot quicker than Nick. After a while, I remember starting to do shots with Gromit, under a very watchful eye from Nick, but once he got confident with me doing Gromit I remember doing Wallace as well. In the museum, where Wallace is yawning, that was the first Wallace's mouth that I did.'

One of the things that's obvious, watching *The Wrong Trousers*, is the love that its makers hold for cinema as a whole. Although there's nothing obvious about

'Hang in there Gromit, everything's under control.'

Wallace's living room wall has three rivet-strewn spacecraft where other people might have ducks – a reminder of his adventure on the Moon in *A Grand Day Out*.

it, particular camera angles and shots bring to mind a series of other movies. The appearance of 'Feathers' McGraw in the doorway of 62 West Wallaby Street, for instance, is modelled on Alec Guinness's arrival in the classic Ealing comedy *The Ladykillers* (1955).

'I remember,' Steve explains, 'during the very long days of shooting the film, Nick and I basically lived at the studio. When we were awake, we were animating. When we had a moment, we would talk about British movies like the Ealing films. *The Ladykillers* – I've always loved that film. It was sinister but innocent. Kooky. Very British, but still exciting.'

Steve has nothing but good memories of his time working on *The Wrong Trousers*. For him it was a magical time.

'I'm absolutely convinced that the feeling of the shoot gets into the fabric of the film. We shot *The Wrong Trousers* in this old studio with a wooden floor where we had to be careful where we stepped, because the floorboards were loose and it would move the camera. There were floorboards cordoned off when we were shooting. It had a very homely, quiet feel to it. There was only Nick and me animating, most of the time. My favourite part of the film is when Gromit is alone in the house, and the penguin comes back. That lovely evening sunlight coming in really reminds me of *The Ladykillers*, and *The Lodger* [1926] by Hitchcock. The whole studio felt like that, so when I watch the film it really brings back memories of the shooting, even though that was tiring. It had the same feel as the film does.'

'No more lodgers. More trouble than they're worth.'

'The bounce has gone from his bungee'
A Close Shave

Opposite: Wallace and Gromit prepare for their big moment: washing Wendolene's windows.

It had been two years since *The Wrong Trousers*, and expectations were riding high. And on Christmas Eve, 1995, those expectations were to be satisfied in a big way with the third Wallace and Gromit film – *A Close Shave*. Despite the fact that their previous two adventures, when added together, wouldn't even make up a full hour, the clay couple had been taken to the heart of the Great British Public in a way that precious few other characters had managed. The BBC, realizing this, had tried to make this a Wallace and Gromit Christmas, to the extent of even commissioning Aardman Animations to make a series of BBC2 logos showing the clay couple in various seasonal situations. Wherever you went, it was hard to miss the fact that *A Close Shave* was going to be shown.

'Well, I don't know. There's something very fishy going on.'

A Close Shave is, in many ways, a simpler, more direct story than *The Wrong Trousers*, but it draws on a list of cinematic influences that are as wide, if not wider. The alert watcher can detect influences from *Brief Encounter* (1945), *The Battle of Britain* (1969), *The Terminator* (1984), *Thunderbirds* (1965) and Steven Spielberg's *Duel* (1971) among others. Production values are obviously sky high: it's rumoured that the short film cost as much as the year's big British cinematic offering, *Trainspotting*.

It's easy to misunderstand the appeal of Wallace and Gromit. Superficially, it's all about a man who makes silly inventions and a dog who gets caught up testing them, isn't it? Actually, no. It's really about how the relationship between the man and the dog keeps getting stretched to breaking point, but never quite snaps. In *The Wrong Trousers* it's the presence of the evil penguin, lodging in Wallace's house, that causes a rift between Wallace and Gromit. In *A Close Shave* the threat to their domestic harmony comes in three forms: the lovely Wendolene, who catches Wallace's eye; the evil Preston, who frames Gromit for a crime he did not commit; and, most insidious of all, Shaun the Sheep, who ends up living with them and changing the dynamic of their relationship for good.

The World of Wallace & Gromit

Above: Gromit sits up in
bed, knitting himself a
warm scarf, when he hears
something odd.

Plot

It's late at night. Wallace is, as so often happens in these adventures, fast
asleep in bed. Gromit is still awake, and is passing the time knitting, but he
looks up when a heavy rumble disturbs the peace of West Wallaby Street,
rattling his teacup and knocking his ball of wool off the bedside table.

Outside the house, a lorry is driving past. Its interior is packed with sheep,
who gaze forlornly out through the lorry's slatted sides at the darkened town.
The lorry stops at a red traffic light at the end of the street, its engine growling
menacingly, but before it can drive off one of the slats breaks
and a small sheep falls out. Curious, and savouring its new-
found freedom, the sheep wanders into Wallace's house
through the dog-flap.

Come the morning, Wallace requests his breakfast
using the push-button alert system he installed some years
ago. He has made some modifications since then: the bed still
tips up and drops him through a trapdoor in the bedroom floor; he still falls
into a pair of trousers with braces and he still has his shirt and jumper
pulled over his head by a small robot; but now, instead of his toast being
flung in the air, a gun fires porridge at him which he has to catch in a bowl.
The machine malfunctions, however, as Wallace's inventions are wont to do,

> **'Porridge today
> Gromit — Tuesday!'**

The World of Wallace & Gromit

Wallace's Inventions: the Porridge Gun

Originally a critical component of the Combined Dressotron and Breakfast Dispenser – in that it went wrong at the critical moment – the porridge gun has been re-engineered as a mobile device that can fire not only porridge (useful for splodging robot dogs) but also soap suds (at dirty windows). A recent upgrade took the porridge gun from one barrel to four, meaning that windows can be cleaned or robot dogs splodged at quadruple the rate.

and just keeps firing porridge at Wallace. He tries desperately to catch it all in bowl while Gromit attempts to fix it, but by the time the canny dog discovers how to switch off the machine, Wallace is covered in porridge and stuck to the wall.

A curious Gromit discovers the source of the problem – the breakfast machine's power cable has been chewed through! Investigating further, Gromit finds a pot plant with a chewed leaf. In the larder, meanwhile, Wallace finds that the bottom of a porridge carton has been chewed away, and a bite has been taken out of his favourite cheese! Sitting down to cogitate on these mysterious occurrences, he is shocked when he sees that a bite has been taken out of his newspaper as well!

Before the two of them can locate whatever bizarre animal is eating its way through the house, the phone rings. It's the owner of the Wool Shop in the High Street – she needs her windows cleaned, and she has heard that Wallace is now running a small business offering just that service: Wallace and Gromit's Wash'n'Go.

All systems go! Gromit pulls a lever which sends Wallace shooting ceilingwards in his armchair. It tips up, sending him sliding down a chute in the wall. He falls into a pair of dungarees and a hard hat, then is deposited in a motorcycle, clutching a bucket and sponge. Gromit, meanwhile, trudges wearily through a door in the wall and climbs into the motorcycle sidecar. Moments later, they're off!

Below: Another of Wallace's inventions malfunctions, and Gromit has to put it right.
Opposite: early plans for the Knit-O-Matic.

'Have you been peckish during the night? Only, someone's been at me cheese!'

Wallace's transfer from living room to motocycle is an affectionate homage to the way the International Rescue crew used to get to their high-tech vehicles in *Thunderbirds*.

The headlines on the *Morning Post* include 'Wool Shortage', 'More Sheep Rustling', 'This Madness Must End' and 'TV Star Homes for £30'. Sports news includes 'Jack Russell Chews Cricket Ball!'

Wallace's Inventions: the Flying Sidecar

Sidecars are tricky things – if they become detached from their motorcycle then they can hurtle, uncontrolled, for miles down roads and over cliffs, threatening passers-by and causing damage to property. Wallace's ingenious solution was to provide the sidecar with wings, a propeller and an engine, allowing its occupant to fly to safety. Also contains an optional mount for the porridge gun.

Wendolene's Wools

WOOL-EWE

WAL
1

The foam in the window washing scene in *A Close Shave* was made using a combination of white hair wax and glass beads (representing the bubbles).

Arriving at the wool shop – Wendolene's Wools – Gromit immediately springs to the top of the ladder, but is taken aback to see a mysterious and large canine figure in the upstairs room – the same figure that was driving the lorry from which the sheep escaped the night before, although Gromit has no way of knowing that. The figure vanishes back behind the curtains, and Gromit returns to work, bungee-falling to the ground, grabbing a bucket and rising back up again to clean the window.

Wallace, meanwhile, enters the shop and meets the owner, Wendolene Ramsbottom, and her dog Preston – a hulking brute with small eyes and a marked glower. Wendolene explains that she was left the shop, and Preston, in her father's will. Wallace can't help but notice that Wendolene has plenty of wool in the shop, despite a local sheep rustling epidemic that has been the main topic of conversation all over town. When he innocently mentions this, she turns rather chilly. Wallace, however, is so taken with Wendolene that he fails to notice Preston leaving the shop and bullying Gromit outside.

After leaving Gromit dangling on the end of his bungee, Preston tracks the missing sheep – the one that fell out of his lorry the night before – to West Wallaby Street. He finds traces of wool in the dog-flap of number 62, and is just about to break in when he is interrupted by Wallace and Gromit's return. Instead, he sneaks down into the coal cellar to continue looking for the sheep.

Entering the house, Wallace and Gromit are shocked to discover that the house has been devastated – almost everything that could be eaten has been eaten! And happily gnawing on a bone in the kitchen they find a small

Opposite: A strangely low tech-solution to the problem of dirty windows. Below: The local town square.

Bob Baker's contributions to the scripts for *The Wrong Trousers* and *A Close Shave* were recognised by the fact that the shop next to 'Wendolene's Wools' is 'Bob the Baker'.

sheep who doesn't look at all embarrassed at being discovered red-hooved.

Instead of getting angry, Wallace rather takes to the sheep and decides to clean him up using one of his many inventions: a combination sheep-dip and sheep-shearing machine located in the basement which goes by the impressive name of Wallace's Knit-O-Matic. Wallace sets the machine to 'wash' but, unsurprisingly, it malfunctions and switches to 'light shave'. Bleating piteously, Shaun (as the sheep has become known) is pulled through a vat of soapy water, squished with sponges and then shaved by a series of clippers on the ends of robot arms. Eventually Shaun is pushed, shivering, from the machine and Wallace is presented with a small jumper made from Shaun's wool.

All of this is observed with great interest by the hidden Preston, who emerges when Wallace and Gromit go upstairs with Shaun. Preston soon finds the plans for the Knit-O-Matic machine, and steals them.

Next day, Wallace and Gromit are busy cleaning the town clock. Wallace has even modified his porridge gun so that it fires soap suds at the clock while Gromit, precariously perched by the clock face, wipes away the dirt.

From his vantage point, Gromit watches as Shaun the Sheep finds his way into Wendolene's house – watched by Preston from the curtained upstairs room. Gromit shins down the ladder to make sure that Shaun is okay – he has a bad feeling about Preston – but when he sticks his head through a hole in the wall to look for Shaun he finds himself in trouble.

Above: An angry Gromit confronts the intruder in the house.
Opposite Top: Gromit is framed, in more ways than one!

'The little chap must be really hungry.'

The World of Wallace & Gromit

'We've tested this on Gromit — haven't we, lad?'

On the other side of the wall, in a room above Wendolene's shop, Preston has arranged a trap. A picture of a butcher holding a cleaver has been pasted on the wall of the room, and by putting his head through the hole Gromit has made it look as if he is the butcher, especially as Shaun is grazing peacefully at the spot where the picture of the cleaver looks like it is about to descend!

Momentarily blinded by the flash as Preston takes a photograph of Gromit's head, the canny canine can't come to Shaun's aid as the sheep is abducted by Preston, along with an entire flock, in the large truck. It's clear that Preston is part of the sheep abductions, but what is his aim? Why are the sheep being abducted? Gromit hears Shaun bleating and gives chase, but although he manages to rescue the sheep from the lorry in a conspicuous act of bravery, Gromit is abducted instead and delivered by Preston to the police station – along with a copy of the incriminating photograph! Gromit is arrested, and locked away as a sheep rustler.

Wallace, saddened by the arrest and incarceration of his canine compatriot, reads the newspapers every day as Gromit's trial progresses. 'Killer Dog Gromit Arrested' reads one, then 'Sheep Dog Trial – Woolygate Continues'. Finally comes the news that Wallace has been dreading – Gromit has been found guilty and sentenced to life imprisonment. Wallace is distraught. It doesn't help matters that his house is full of sheep and his inventions are breaking down around him. How will he survive without Gromit?

A Close Shave

Above: Wallace and the flock read with horror of Gromit's fate.
Left: Gromit's cell, once the home of a smaller, more avian prisoner.
Opposite Top: What the flock is going on?

The 5000-piece jigsaw puzzle that Gromit ends up making while in his cell actually contains 104 pieces.

The World of Wallace & Gromit

In the midst of Wallace's misery, he gets a visit from Wendolene. She consoles him over Gromit's conviction, but tells him to stay away from her shop. 'Forget me,' she says, 'I'm no good for you.'

Gromit, meanwhile, is sent to jail. Ironically, he is incarcerated in the cell previously occupied by his arch nemesis, 'Feathers' McGraw.

Shortly after Gromit arrives in prison, a package arrives for him. It's a 5000-piece jigsaw puzzle. The thought of having enough time to complete a puzzle that size almost sends him into despair, but when he finally steels himself to put the puzzle together he finds a message scrawled across it, that says: 'Friday Night, 8pm, Be Ready, A Friend'.

Gromit checks the time and date. It's Friday and it's 8pm. Before he can even draw breath, the bars on his cell window have been cut away by Shaun the sheep, using a circular saw. Shaun is perched on the shoulders of a tower of sheep, all of whom are perched on Wallace's shoulders. It's a jail break!

When they're a safe distance away from the prison, Wallace suggests to Gromit that he might want to go abroad until the search for him has died down. However, before they can implement the plan they discover Wendolene and Preston abducting their sheep in a truck. The two of them are obviously the *real* sheep rustlers – probably so they can shear the sheep and provide wool for Wendolene's shop. Wallace and Gromit overhear Wendolene objecting to Preston's rough approach, to which he responds by throwing her into the back of the truck as well.

'Let me out,' cries Wendolene. 'You're not going to turn me into dog meat!'

Shocked at this unexpected turn of events, Wallace and Gromit chase after the truck in the motorcycle-sidecar combination that Wallace has thoughtfully brought with him, but Preston sees them giving chase, manages to get behind them and tries to run them off the road. Fortunately, the quick-thinking Gromit erects the window-cleaning ladder, climbs up it while the lorry is gaining on them, grabs an overhead power line and hoists the entire motorcycle and sidecar off the road, swinging them in a complete circle which ends up with them behind the lorry again!

> **'You'll be hunted down, like ... well, a dog.'**

Wallace accelerates toward the escaping lorry, but suddenly the connecting pin comes out of the arm holding the sidecar to the motorcycle and the sidecar detaches, running off under its own steam with Gromit trapped inside. It swerves towards a cliff-edge and plunges over the edge of a 2000-ft drop … and turns into an aeroplane when two stubby wings emerge from its sides. Good old Wallace – his inventions always come through in the end.

Meanwhile, Wallace has managed to catch up with the lorry and undo the door at the back. The sheep manage to scramble across him and end up on the motorbike with him. Alas, Preston brakes hard and all the sheep end up back in the truck.

Opposite: High jinks on a motorbike with Gromit disguised as a scarecrow, and an all-sheep display team.

Preston arrives at Wendolene's Wool Shop and drives the lorry through a secret entrance and into a huge area where strange machines loom. The sheep are herded into a huge metal hopper which feeds into Preston's own Knit-O-Matic Machine – which has obviously been nicked from Wallace's designs. Wallace is about to be sucked into the machine with the sheep, but Shaun alerts Gromit to their location by flashing the lights on a nearby chimney, and Gromit bursts into the sheep-processing area in his sidecar-aircraft.

Gromit and Preston confront one another. Preston gets covered in porridge fired out of the sidecar's window-cleaning gun and falls into the Knit-O-Matic Machine. Wallace assumes that it's all over for the brutal mutt, but Wendolene reveals that Preston is a cyberdog – a robotic canine invented by her father. It'll take more than a Knit-O-Matic machine to finish him!

'Ohh! Get yourselves organised down there!'

Preston bursts out of the machine, shorn of all vestiges of his dog disguise, and activates his Mutton-O-Matic Machine – a monstrosity which is designed to turn sheep into tins of dog food! That's what the sheep-rustling has been leading to – originally it was a means of furnishing Wendolene with enough wool to stock her shop, but Preston has discovered a use for the shorn sheep!

Everyone ends up on the conveyor belt that leads into the mechanical jaws of the Mutton-O-Matic, desperately attempting to evade its spinning wheels. Fortunately, Preston is knocked into the machine by Shaun the sheep, and jams the entire thing. Wallace, Gromit, Wendolene and the sheep are saved, and Preston is turned back into his constituent cogs and springs, all neatly canned.

'Feathers' McGraw appears in one shot in *A Close Shave*, but nobody outside Aardman has yet spotted him!

Days later, Gromit is pardoned, and he and Wallace return to West Wallaby Street. Wallace has rebuilt Preston as a smaller dog on wheels, with all the aggressive tendencies taken out. Wendolene pops round to thank him, and Wallace takes the opportunity to ask her in for a bit of cheese. He is devastated, however, when she tells him that she doesn't like cheese.

Still, as he says, that leaves more for him and Gromit!

Behind the scenes

If the team at Aardman thought there was pressure on them to follow up *A Grand Day Out*, that was nothing compared to the pressure on them to provide a successor to *The Wrong Trousers*. Britain, indeed the world, had taken Wallace and Gromit to its heart.

Steve Box, who had worked as assistant animator on *The Wrong Trousers*, was keen to crack on with a new Wallace and Gromit TV film.

'As soon as we'd finished *The Wrong Trousers* I remember saying to Nick, "Let's do another one!"' Steve recalls, 'and, after he'd had a rest, he wanted to. I was always going to work on it, but I wasn't involved at all with the writing and development: it wasn't 'til it was story-boarded that I started to get involved.'

Given the huge success of *The Wrong Trousers*, it would have been foolish in the extreme to split up the team that had made it happen, and so Bob Baker was immediately invited back to help Nick Park write the script.

'Nick said, "Well, I'd love to do something about a sheep",' Bob recalls, 'because he always had a picture of a sheep in the background of the first two films. And so I thought "sheep …" and we gradually built up the story.'

Bob Baker had always insisted that the reason people loved Wallace and Gromit had less to do with the inventions and eccentricity and more to do with the emotional relationship

'That's my machine — I've got Patent Pending on that!'

94

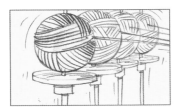   

between the characters. For that reason, he had a clear idea of what the new film should be about.

'We wanted to make it a love story,' he says. 'We wanted Wallace to have an emotional encounter with a lady. To keep the "British" feel to it, we used as a kind of model the film *Brief Encounter*, though we also watched lots of other movie. We generally worked very hard.'

Bob did find that the way he and Nick worked together was different from the approach on *The Wrong Trousers*. Partly this was because Nick had used up most of the ideas in his notebook on the previous film, and had yet to recharge his creative batteries. For that reason, they looked further afield for inspiration.

'It took a little bit longer than *The Wrong Trousers*,' Bob says, 'because we took longer working out the story. There were a lot more meetings where we just let ideas fly around, rather than getting down to the nitty-gritty. There was a steadier approach to it, because we had to start from scratch. There was the sheep on the wall, and the idea that we wanted to pose a threat to the Wallace and Gromit relationship, like Wallace falling for somebody else. That was it.'

There was, perhaps unsurprisingly, a certain amount of material which was originally written by Bob and Nick, but later cut out as they refined the story and shaped it into a half-hour form.

'We played around with Wendolene quite a bit,' Bob reveals. 'She was going to be living in the manor house, and her father was an inventor who had lost all their money. In the original concept we started building it up that he was in the background somewhere. She thought she'd lost her father but in fact he'd been kidnapped or something. Then we sort of went off that into the rustling story, which had more soul to it somehow. A robot dog rustling sheep for wool! It's mad; it's lovely and mad, isn't it?'

Having said that, Bob still felt that *A Close Shave* contained all the right elements for a stunning adventure.

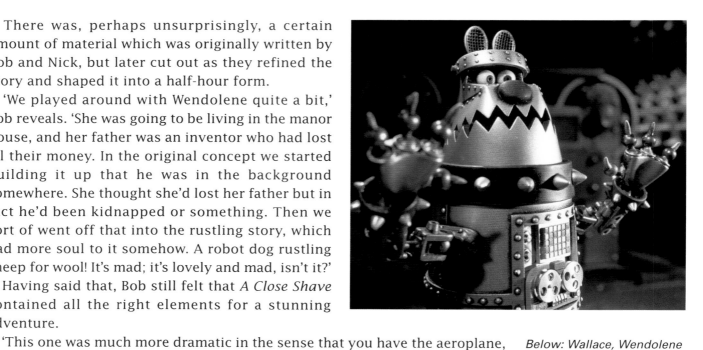

'This one was much more dramatic in the sense that you have the aeroplane, and the chase, and the sheep. Nick would just do a drawing of sheep on a motorbike and you'd think, 'Wow, that's fantastic!' And the window cleaning! I don't know where that came from, but it's just lovely, I mean it's just beautiful.'

Steve Box was also aware that *A Close Shave* had a different feel about it to its predecessor.

Below: Wallace, Wendolene and the flock run from the robot Preston and the rotating jaws of the Mutton-O-Matic.

'It was a very different experience,' he admits. 'It was a bigger crew. The production was scaled up. The idea was to shoot it slightly quicker. It was a more elaborate story with a few more characters in. We had about seven animators, and a production manager. We didn't have any of that on *The Wrong Trousers*.'

With other people doing the animation, and Nick Park directing their efforts, the man who had invented Wallace and Gromit found that he had almost no time to animate the characters himself. In fact, *A Close Shave* was the last time that Nick Park actually did any animation.

'On *A Close Shave*,' Nick reveals, 'I finally got round to doing some animation about four or five o'clock in the day, and I'd get about half a second done a day. It was very stressful, trying to do the animation as well as directing. But I find it very important to get my hands on the characters, to actually do the final tweaks to get the right look so that they're from the same world, and the same mind.'

This attempt to get everything looking as if it came from the same world and the same mind led Nick to find ways of ensuring that all the animators in his team were working in the same way, rather than imposing their own creative ideas on what he wanted.

'With Wallace and Gromit,' David Sproxton, one of Aardman's founders states, 'it's a bit like taking over a role from a well-known actor on a soap. Nick would organize master classes with the animators, and say, "This is how Wallace behaves, this

Ann Reid, who provided Wendolene's voice, was one of the regular characters in Victoria Woods's TV comedy *dinnerladies*.

'It's a sheep-mincing thing! Now that's clever!'

PRESTON'S MUTTON-O-MATIC

is how Gromit behaves, these are his key movements, these are his key gestures." And he'd try to get the animators to fit into a mould.'

'I've never felt I've lost control,' Nick says now, 'but the more people you have, the more people you have to direct, so the less you have to do yourself. I felt not out of control but less 'hands on'. I'm used to directing now, and I like making big films, but there's a certain sacrifice you make. A lot of time on set is spent asking somebody to do something exactly as you want it. I'm very exact about what I want, which is very tiring for people, I think, but people love giving you what you want as well.'

'On *A Close Shave*, I was doing Wendolene and the whole wool shop – the whole romance,' says Steve Box. 'I wanted to get more into the characters and the acting, which I particularly love, and which I think is a crucial part. The wool shop sequence followed the storyboards of course, and the dialogue was pre-recorded, but I very much had a hand in where the camera was and how things were staged. I think that was a great relief to Nick, because he continued to try to animate but obviously had people wanting to ask him questions all day long. With seven or eight people animating, it was a great relief to him that he could leave me to get on with it.'

'I always felt that, throughout the three films, it's what naturally happens

Above: Wallace is torn between rescuing Wendolene and admiring Preston's ingenuity. Opposite: A Close Shave finishes as all good adventures should, with the hero sitting at home reflecting on what has happened.

The World of Wallace & Gromit

when you have more people working on something,' Nick admits ruefully. 'I've got a great crew, a great team that is very skilful, but something happens when there's a lot of people. Things get naturally slicker and the animation gets smoother and the finish gets even smoother. It happened to a degree on *A Close Shave*. The animation in some ways got a little more conservative as well. It didn't quite have the boldness that I wanted. There are chases and surprises, but that's not what Wallace and Gromit are about. It's something more slow-going and ritualistic: tea-making, that kind of thing.'

'*The Wrong Trousers* – we always look to that as the benchmark,' Nick says. 'The story fit really well into the time. With *A Close Shave* we were cutting corners in places, telling the story a bit too economically. There were a lot more strands in *A Close Shave* to tie up, and characters to pay off. I thought there were some strong ideas in it, but the story wasn't as strong as *The Wrong Trousers*.'

Despite the general feeling that *A Close Shave* hadn't quite achieved its aims, the general reaction from the great British public was one of total, unalloyed pleasure.

'And what happened?' Bob Baker asks. 'It won another Oscar! You can't say fairer than that, can you?'

Gromit is seen reading *The Telegruff*, whose headline is 'Even More Sheep Rustling!' and the *Daily Lamp-Post*, whose back page headline is 'Marrow Sets New Speed Record'.

'The Edam is stranded'

Wallace & Gromit's Cracking Contraptions

Following the TV transmission of *A Close Shave*, there was an obvious and continuing demand for Wallace and Gromit. However, David Sproxton, Peter Lord and Nick Park were reluctant to do anything straight away (not that 'straight away' has the same meaning when applied to stop-motion animation as it does to anything else). They felt strongly that it was time to expand Aardman's range by moving into the cinema. And so the next five years or so saw them developing the movie *Chicken Run* in conjunction with Hollywood's DreamWorks studio, for eventual release in 2000. But Wallace and Gromit just refused to go away.

Following the huge national and international success of *Chicken Run* Aardman as a whole spent some time discussing what to do next. The company eventually decided that the best thing it could do would be to give the public what they kept on saying they wanted – more Wallace and Gromit. And so production started on what was initially called *The Great Vegetable Plot* but soon became *Wallace & Gromit Curse of the WereRabbit*.

'Oh, now that's just not cricket, Gromit!'

However, in order to whet the public appetite, it was decided that a series of very short films should be made. And so *Wallace and Gromit's Cracking Contraptions* debuted first on the Internet (a medium that was in its infancy when *A Grand Day Out* was first transmitted), and then later on the BBC in Christmas 2002.

The Soccamatic

It's a lazy summer's afternoon in West Wallaby Street, and Wallace and Gromit are making the most of the warmth and the sunshine. Temporarily abandoning their fridge full of cheese and their cupboards of crackers, they've headed out to the local playing field where Wallace, resplendent in his 1950s-vintage football strip, is punting balls towards his loyal canine goalkeeper, who is dressed in a green jersey and red gloves. It's all just a bit of harmless fun – until Wallace realizes that Gromit's a lot better at the game than he is, and is catching all the balls. With ease.

Unwilling to be outshone by his own dog, Wallace wheels his latest invention onto the pitch – the Preston North End Soccamatic Machine (named after his favourite football team). It's an automated ball-deliverer and kicker, and it sends hundreds of footballs zooming toward Gromit like cannonballs. Gromit, sensible dog that he is, ducks.

The Soccamatic Machine soon runs out of balls, but Wallace isn't worried. Not when he has an automatic reloader ready to shovel new balls in at the flick of a switch.

Gromit looks on in horror. This thing could run forever if it isn't stopped!

Wallace is shocked, however, when Gromit deploys his own invention – an inflatable goalkeeper's vest and gloves which fill the entire goalmouth. Now the balls will just bounce off. It's a score draw.

'Anyone for tennis, perchance?'

The Snoozatron

Wallace is in bed. It's three o'clock in the morning and he can't get to sleep. He tosses and turns, but to no avail. He's wide awake. Perhaps he ate too much cheese for supper.

Finally, Wallace gives up. Reaching out a hand into the cold bedroom air, he presses a button.

In Gromit's room, a loud alarm jerks the dog from deep sleep to instant wakefulness. Gromit knows what's coming. It's time once again for him to play his role in his Master's latest bizarre invention – the Snoozatron.

In Wallace's bedroom, automated arms emerge from concealed hatches in the walls and make him comfortable, plumping up the bed and the pillow. A crane drops a hot water bottle on the bed. Another crane arm deposits a teddy bear in Wallace's arms. He snuggles deeper into the counterpane, feeling more relaxed.

Gromit, meanwhile, has put on a sheep suit and is trudging downstairs, still half-asleep.

In Wallace's bedroom, a gramophone emerges from a hidden compartment behind a picture on the wall and starts playing soothing music. Wallace feels his eyelids beginning to grow heavy – but there's still one more thing that needs to happen before he can fall asleep properly …

Above: Wallace settles down to sleep, but for Gromit it's a dog's life. Opposite: Wallace's Snowmanotron menaces Gromit's rather more artistic endeavour.

'I'll never sleep after all that cheese.'

The World of Wallace & Gromit

In the kitchen, Gromit – in his sheep costume – adopts a position in the middle of the floor, arms outstretched. He's clearly waiting for something, and he's not too pleased about it either. Suddenly, a massive spring propels him high into the air, through a hidden trapdoor in the ceiling and directly into Wallace's bedroom where he hangs in the air for a few seconds before dropping back down through the trapdoor and back into the kitchen again.

In Wallace's bedroom, a mechanical counter clicks from 500 to 499. Wallace's automated sheep-counting mechanism begins its work, and as Gromit appears through the trapdoor again, Wallace begins to drift off. But Gromit knows that he's got some time left to go before he can head back to bed, so he picks up his newspaper and begins to read.

The Snowmanotron

It's almost Christmas. Snow covers the roofs of West Wallaby Street, but inside Number 62 it's warm and snug.

Reading the paper one morning over breakfast, Gromit discovers that a grand snowman competition is to be held in the town. Enthused, and determined to win, he rushes outside and creates his entry – a lovingly crafted snowman bearing a distinct resemblance to Rodin's famous statue The Thinker.

Before Gromit can enter his snowman in the competition, Wallace drives up to the front door of the house in his latest invention – a Snowmanotron. A snowplough in front of the

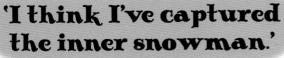

'I think I've captured the inner snowman.'

'**Well done, Gromit, but I thought that snowman was abominable!**'

device channels snow to where mechanical arms can shovel it into a large hopper that leads to a refrigerator. Inside the refrigerator, more arms compress and shape the snow into what will hopefully be an award-winning snowperson.

Alas, when the door of Wallace's Snowmanotron opens, revealing his rather crude entry, it accidentally crushes Gromit's own rather more artistic version. Gromit gives up in disgust and stalks back into the house, slamming the front door behind him.

The vibration of the front door causes snow from the roof to slide off and fall onto Wallace like a mini-avalanche. Gromit re-emerges to find out what all the fuss is about. Seeing what he thinks is a new and rather better snowman on the front path, he picks up a couple of stones and gives the snowman two eyes and a nose. Gromit wins the competition, and Wallace is left to defrost slowly from his frozen state.

The World of Wallace & Gromit

The Autochef

Opposite: Gromit gets a prize, but Wallace just gets a chill.
Opposite bottom: Somewhere inside that snowman is a frozen inventor!
Below: A bright-eyed Wallace prepares to demonstrate his latest food-processing invention, but Gromit isn't convinced it will work.

It's breakfast-time at 62 West Wallaby Street – traditionally, not a good time if a dog wants some peace and quiet to read his newspaper and eat a banana. This breakfast is no exception. Wallace has been working solidly through the night, and wants to demonstrate the fruits of his labours to Gromit.

Gromit pulls on a set of waterproofs. He knows what's coming.

Activated by Wallace's remote control, a robot rolls into the dining room. It's obviously some kind of mechanical chef, judging by the blender sticking out of the top of its head.

Gromit obviously has a bad feeling about this, but Wallace – oblivious to Gromit's concerns – orders scrambled eggs.

After a few moments of frantic cooking, the robot serves the scrambled eggs – vertically into the air. They land on Gromit's head.

Undeterred, Wallace asks the robot for fried eggs. The frying pan is hidden under the robot's head, and the mechanical chef sets to work cooking the eggs to Wallace's satisfaction.

This time the cooked eggs are tossed straight at Wallace, covering

> 'I think I'll have the Continental tomorrow, lad!'

The robot in 'The Autochef' episode of *Cracking Contraptions* is only the third speaking part in the whole Wallace and Gromit TV canon (the others are Wallace and Wendolene, of course).

his eyes so he can't see what the robot is up to. And, more to the point, he can't find the remote control to turn it off.

A spout emerges from robot's nose, spraying tea everywhere. The robot starts shouting nonsense. Gromit, tiring of having his breakfast everywhere apart from the table, stuffs his banana over the spout. The robot explodes.

'More tea, Vicar? Get off and milk it! More stuffing, madam? Something for the weekend, sir? Knickers!'

The Bully-Proof Vest

It's late. Lightning flashes, casting dark shadows on the wall. Peals of thunder shake the house, rattling the crockery. Wind, gusting through a partially opened window, slams doors violently. Somewhere outside, a cat screeches.

Wallace is pouring out a cup of tea in his kitchen. The storm has made him nervous, and his hand shakes, rattling the cup. As he leaves the kitchen with his cup of tea and a box of crackers he is oblivious to the shadowy figure that scuttles across a doorway behind him.

Entering the living room, Wallace's attention is distracted for a moment, and the shadowy figure steals a cracker from his hand.

Realizing that his cracker has been hijacked, Wallace turns round and confronts the mysterious figure. It's Gromit, in a black sweater and balaclava, making Ninja moves with a rolling pin.

The sight should have sent Wallace into deep shock, but instead he deploys his latest invention – the Bully-Proof Vest. It's a button-operated box on his chest that sends a boxing glove propelled through the air on the end of a spring. A powerful spring. A spring so powerful, in fact, that it pushes Gromit across the room and through a door, and gives him a black eye into the bargain, which is a bit unfair considering that he was only taking part in Wallace's experiment to help his master out.

Satisfied with the test, Wallace winds the boxing glove back into box. Turning to leave the room, he accidentally trips and falls. The button on the Bully-Proof Vest hits the floor and activates itself, projecting Wallace into air and smashing him into the ceiling.

'You'd better get a ladder, Gromit — I think I've cracked me Artex.'

Wallace has a picture on his wall of a hunk of cheese, with the legend 'N'est-ce pas un fromage' – an homage to the Belgian surrealist artist Rene Magritte who painted a pipe and wrote beneath it (in French, of course) 'This is not a pipe'.

Shopper 13

Above and below: Beautiful miniature props from the Shopper 13 episode. Overleaf: The Bully-Proof vest in action.

In a futuristic control room somewhere deep beneath West Wallaby Street, Wallace and Gromit are hunched over consoles of switches and buttons. After a tension-filled pre-launch sequence, Wallace's latest labour-saving device is released upon an unsuspecting world – an automated shopping robot.

The robot – Shopper 13 – is guided via remote control on its way to the nearby Pack'n'Save shop. Once inside, Gromit directs it to the cheese shelves, where it retrieves a giant Edam with its robotic hands. Alas, the weight of the cheese causes an overload, and Shopper 13 suddenly veers off course, its wheels wobbling wildly.

'Begin cheese acquisition, aisle two.'

Shopper 13 makes its way uncertainly back towards West Wallaby Street, but things are progressing from bad to worse. The uneven weight distribution is throwing the entire mechanism out of whack, and eventually a wheel falls off, causing the robot to go in circles. A clever manoeuvre with a baguette, which the robot uses as a crutch, gets it going in a straight line again, but it's grievously wounded now.

The robot's other wheel falls off just as it gets to the door of Wallace's house. Shopper 13 collapses, finally defeated, and the Edam rolls away down to the bottom of the garden.

But all is not lost! Wallace deploys his emergency retrieval system – Shaun the Sheep! Shaun trots off to the end of the garden, but instead of bringing the cheese back to the control room he eats it instead.

The title and general style of this episode refer to the film *Apollo 13*, which tells the true story of an American space mission which goes wrong.

The Tellyscope

Wallace and Gromit are comfortably ensconced in their chairs, waiting for their favourite TV programme to come on – *The Cheese Files*. Unwilling to get up out of his chair and walk to the TV to turn it to the right channel, Wallace uses his new remote control device. A tennis ball, fired from the arm of his chair, plunges through a hole in the wall and rolls down a long, spiral track made of drainpipe sections. The ball is carried through a half-circle by rotating arms, and is then kicked away by a mechanical leg. It falls into a gloved

Opposite: Shopper 13, using its loaf.

Above and below: Wallace's Tellyscope brings TV to his fingertips.

mechanical hand which, set in motion by the weight of the ball, now acts as a lever, operating a mechanism.

And up in the living room, the TV is pushed on castors across the room until Wallace can push the button for the right channel. The TV set slowly returns to its optimal watching position, and Wallace and Gromit settle down in their chairs.

But sadly, Wallace has pushed the wrong button. A different programme comes on – one which brings back some terrifying memories of psychopathic penguin criminals. Worse – Wallace has run out of tennis balls and can't repeat the process! With a long-suffering look, Gromit hands him a TV remote instead, but Wallace – not understanding what it is – uses it in place of a

'That's torn it — I think I've bent my tube!'

One programme on TV is guaranteed to bring back un-welcome memories for Wallace and Gromit – *When Penguins Turn!*

tennis ball, firing it across the room and letting it work its way through the complicated machinery. Which, because of its rectangular shape, it completely destroys. The TV then blows up in sympathy.

Opposite: Gromit rides a wild vacuum cleaner. Overleaf: Gromit begins to suspect he's not going to get any dinner – again.

The Turbo Diner

Unusually for him, Wallace has returned to the scene of one of his earlier less-than-triumphant moments, and is attempting to repair the autochef that made such a hash of his and Gromit's breakfasts. Come dinnertime, Wallace is still repairing the robot, but he tells Gromit not to worry – his Turbo Diner will take care of everything. Beaming contentedly, he reaches over to the wall and pops a coin in a large meter.

Manacles snap across Wallace and Gromit's wrists, fastening them to their chairs. Ropes pull the chairs closer to the table. A hatch opens in the ceiling and a huge metal hood is lowered down. Within moments, a vacuum sucks everything off the table, and a new, steaming hot dinner is laid in its place. A flamethrower lights the candles on the table. It's perfection.

And then the meter runs out. Wallace and Gromit, still in manacles, can't reach the table. Or the meter. They're stuck, gazing forlornly at a beautiful meal.

The 525 Crackervac

Wallace has developed a robotic vacuum cleaner on wheels but – like many of his creations – it goes rapidly out of control. Apparently it wants his crackers, but Wallace isn't prepared to relinquish them without a fight.

The Crackervac's metal teeth glint dangerously.

Wallace throws the crackers to Gromit.

It's a Mexican stand-off – one broken only when Gromit throws a cracker into the air. The robot makes a dive for it and Gromit lassos it in mid-air. Gromit launches himself at the robot, grasping its midsection with his legs and holding on for all he's worth. The robot goes mad, bucking and broncking around the room in a desperate attempt to dislodge Gromit. Eventually its bag bursts, covering Wallace in dust.

The title of this episode – 'The 525 Crackervac' – is a neat nod towards 1960s and 1970s kids' TV programme *Crackerjack*, the catchphrase of which was: 'It's Friday, it's five twenty-five and it's *Crackerjack!*'

'That's three hundred horsepower of pure suck. Not bad, eh?'

Below and opposite: Gromit poses for the annual exchange of greetings cards (nothing for 'Feathers' McGraw or Preston, of course).

A Christmas Cardomatic

Gromit, dressed uncomfortably as a rather large and plump robin, is standing in front of a roller blind showing a snowy Christmas scene. As he adopts various poses, Wallace takes a set of photographs with his Christmas Cardomatic Machine – a camera connected to a developing machine and a production line. Within moments, a range of Christmas cards emerges from the machine – some better than others.

Satisfied with his cards, Wallace allows the roller blind to roll back up into the ceiling. Ironically, the scene outside is far more Christmassy than the one on the backdrop.

Behind the scenes

There was no way, following the rapturous reception of *A Close Shave*, that Wallace and Gromit could be allowed to lie idle.

'There was an idea to do a short film, round about seven or eight minutes long,' says Steve Box, who worked with Nick on both *The Wrong Trousers* and *A Close Shave*. 'The idea was that maybe I would do it. Nick was right in the thick of *Chicken Run* then. We met – me and Nick and Bob Baker – and we came up with an idea about Wallace's mother coming to visit. I worked on it for a good long time. I actually storyboarded the whole thing, but it kind of died the death. Trying to attempt something without Nick was just so difficult.'

Just the idea of Wallace's mother is enough to send any Wallace and Gromit fan into a frenzy. The plot, as far as it was developed, promised to be on a par with *The Wrong Trousers* and *A Close Shave*, as Steve Box goes on to explain.

The World of Wallace & Gromit

'Wallace was expecting his mother, and this terrible woman turns up and puts Gromit through hell. She's a complete cleanliness freak, and she even has this bag that seals around Gromit to keep dog smells in. Poor Gromit puts up with the whole thing because he thinks she is Wallace's mother, but then Wallace's real mother arrives at the end, and we discover that this woman is some kind of cleaning equipment saleswoman, so Gromit endured all this hardship and was absolutely furious at the end. It would end with this dark look from Gromit, and Wallace looking apologetic.'

There would, of course, have been some interesting creative decisions.

'The difficult thing was whether we should see Wallace's mother,' Steve says. 'That was tricky.'

The idea of a film of any length was quietly shelved when it became clear that, as Nick Park would need to be involved on the creative side, they could not proceed until he had completed work on *Chicken Run*. However, people just kept on asking when Wallace and Gromit would be back. That in itself was a force pushing Aardman towards producing some kind of follow-up to *A Close Shave*, as Nick Park explains:

'The Japanese had been to us saying, 'We can't wait for the feature film! We need more Wallace and Gromit, otherwise it's going to dry up in Japan!' That's what sparked it off really. They were saying, 'Is there any way you can give us really short pieces with them, for playing on TV in Japan?' so we came up with the idea of *Wallace and Gromit's Cracking Contraptions*.'

'We'd already done Wallace and Gromit covers for a scientific magazine for kids,' David Sproxton, one of Aardman's co-founders explains, 'and we'd provided twelve stills of silly inventions for a calendar, and when the Japanese said they wanted more material, I thought, "Well, how long do you need? How long can these things be? About a minute or so?" and they said, "Actually, that'll be fine." "What can we do", we thought, "that isn't going to need an awful lot of scriptwriting?" because that's the bit that takes the time. Well, why don't we animate those twelve calendar ideas? Nick has thought through the basics. They'll need a bit of story wrapped around them, but basically the idea is that Wallace makes a machine that goes horribly wrong. So we actually ran a competition in-house for scripts, based on that idea.'

'**Everything seems to be developing nicely.**'

As well as satiating the general desire for more Wallace and Gromit, especially in Japan, the management at Aardman could see another reason for going ahead with *Cracking Contraptions*. It had been decided that the follow-up to *Chicken Run* should be what everyone wanted – a Wallace and Gromit movie. The problem was that not only would it take some time to write and storyboard, but there were only a few key animators at Aardman who had any experience of working on the pair.

'It served two purposes,' says David Sproxton. 'One was to have some material to put out because there hadn't been anything new for years and it kept the thing alive, and the other point was it was a very good training ground for the animators to refresh themselves. And it wasn't going to eat too much into Nick and Steve's time: Christopher Sadler and Loyd Price directed the pieces.'

'*Cracking Contraptions* was a good way to train directors and get animators ready,' Nick Park confirms. 'That would be a benefit of it for the feature film.'

Of course, although the idea was that Nick would take more of a back seat this time, it didn't quite work out that way.

'Overseeing it all was quite a big thing,' he laughs. 'There's a lot to oversee – there's the scripts, the jokes, making sure that it all ties in with the characters, making sure that the models actually look like Wallace and Gromit, that the animation has the right feel, the sets look good ...'

Following the falling apart of his seven-minute 'Wallace's Mother' idea, Steve Box was keen to contribute to *Cracking Contraptions*.

'Nick had already done some drawings of inventions,' he recalls, 'and the idea was to make them into this series of short one-minute films, so some of the scripts were based on those. Some of them didn't really work as films. They were more like pictorial gags, so the animators and the directors were given the opportunity to come up with their own ideas. I met them often to see what they were doing, to see if it was appropriate, and maybe to help them structure things. They all had great ideas, so it was just advice really. Apart from that, I did a couple of shots in the "Snoozatron". It was really lovely because I haven't animated for quite a while, and I did the shot of Gromit walking down the stairs looking sleepy. For the first ten frames I could hardly remember what I was

Above: Outside Wallace's window, the view is breathtaking.
Opposite: Wallace finally realises that nothing can compare with reality.

The World of Wallace & Gromit

doing, and then all of a sudden it was like I was with Gromit again, like finding an old friend. I so enjoyed it, and I do so miss it now.'

Watching the way that other animators handled the characters, Steve Box – who already knew that he would be co-directing the Wallace and Gromit movie with Nick Park – was already working out who to bring on board.

'Some people's work is subtler than others. Wallace might be smaller or tighter in his movements, slightly more conservative. To that person you'd say, "Push it a bit more, it's all a bit tight." Someone else might be much more wild and push too far and lose the shape of the brow, and maybe not have the subtlety that he needs. It's very difficult. It takes years to understand Wallace exactly but Nick and I have now animated him for years, and he's evolved as well, so he's not the same as he was in *A Grand Day Out*. It's all down to performance: if you *believe* that the character is thinking, then we're flexible on whether the shape of the brow or the length of the leg is exactly right. What counts is whether it is a good performance.'

'It's Apocalypse Chow!'
Wallace & Gromit go global

Three years between *A Grand Day Out* and *The Wrong Trousers*. Two years between *The Wrong Trousers* and *A Close Shave*. Seven years between *A Close Shave* and *Wallace and Gromit's Cracking Contraptions*. Each appearance of the innocent inventor and his cynical canine is lovingly crafted and hand-polished, released like a collectors' piece.

And yet there have been other sightings. Fleeting TV appearances and tasters, to whet our appetites for the main courses to come. Over the years Wallace and Gromit have appeared in a small number of slick adverts – some of which have only ever been seen abroad – and have even become part of BBC2's Christmas celebrations.

Aardman have had strong connections with the British advertising industry for many years. Indeed, it would be hard to find a time when there wasn't at least one of their commercials running on TV, from the Scotch tape skeleton dancing in his living room to the more recent PG Tips birds sharing a flat.

The reason that the British advertising industry keep going back to Aardman is precisely the reason the British public do – the feeling of comfort and character that Aardman's animators manage to imbue in all of their creations. In an industry where slick, computer-generated images are rampant, there's something cosy, almost reassuring about what they do. It has the feeling of something hand-crafted rather than mass-produced.

Although Aardman were keen to expand their commercial business, they were markedly reluctant to exploit Wallace and Gromit. The clay companions were protected, despite the continual requests for them to promote someone's goods.

'From 1995 to 1998 we were offered every TV ad in the book,' explains Arthur Sheriff, Aardman's chief publicist. 'You name it, we were offered it, from mobile phones to DIY companies to the obvious foods and drinks that feature within the films, and we turned them all down because of integrity. We wanted to keep the integrity of Wallace and Gromit. We see it every

The World of Wallace & Gromit

day – a trend comes along and suddenly that trend is everywhere, from cornflake packets to whatever, and it loses its credibility very quickly. We don't want to be a Ninja Turtles.'

That's not to say that Wallace and Gromit have never appeared in commercials, it's just that Aardman have been amazingly selective about what they chose to do. And where they chose to do it. In common with film stars such as Harrison Ford, Richard Gere and Sean Connery, Wallace and Gromit's first appearance in a commercial was, in fact, in the land of the Rising Sun. *A Grand Day Out*, *The Wrong Trousers* and *A Close Shave* had already proved a huge hit with Japanese audiences, and as a result the snack manufacturer Glico (responsible for such appetizing fare as Collon Crème, Giant Rainbow Pocky and Kittyland Cookies) commissioned Aardman to make three commercials for them. The product advertised by the pair was Glico's Putchin pudding – something like a crème caramel.

The first Glico commercial is effectively a dance routine, with Wallace, Gromit and a flock of sheep grooving on down to a Japanese pop song extolling the benefits of Glico's Putchin pudding. Sheep appear through serving hatches, Gromit is in sunglasses boogying like an expert and Wallace is doing his best to appear cool. The commercial reflects *A Close Shave* in

Right: Sheep dreams.

its depiction of Wallace's house occupied by a flock of sheep.

The second Glico commercial is more plot-driven, with Shaun the Sheep sleeping peacefully in a meadow and suddenly being awakened by the distinctive sound of Wallace and Gromit opening a Putchin pudding in their kitchen. The advert cuts rapidly between Wallace's spoon as it gets closer and closer to the surface of the pudding and Shaun as he races towards the house, first on foot, then on a bicycle and finally swinging on a rope and bursting through the kitchen window, just in time to snatch the pudding from a surprised Wallace and eat it.

The third Glico commercial harks back to the halcyon days of *A Grand Day Out*. Wallace and Gromit have travelled to the Moon for a picnic in their big, orange rocket but, even through the cold vacuum of space, Shaun can hear them opening a Putchin pudding. Grabbing his crash helmet, Shaun leaps into a single-sheep rocket ship and blasts through the atmosphere. Heading for the Moon, he dodges through a meteor shower, smashing one of his rocket engines in the process. His craft spirals out of control towards the Moon's surface, and Shaun is forced to bail out.

Wallace and Gromit are distracted from their pudding by the distant explosion as the rocket ship hits the Moon's surface, but when they turn back they find Shaun safe and sound, happily eating their pudding with the folds of his parachute settling around him.

Glico weren't the only company to wish to use Wallace and Gromit in their advertising campaigns. Aardman had already forged an alliance with Sumitomo – the second largest insurance company in Japan – and Sumitomo commissioned the plasticine pair for a short commercial showing the kinds of things that insurance policies protect against. In the commercial, Wallace and Gromit are driving along on their motorcycle, along with a stunt team of sheep, when they accidentally run over a tortoise (bearing a stunning resemblance to Frank the Tortoise from Nick Park's original *Creature Comforts*). The sheep are thrown into the air with Wallace and Gromit, but they all manage to land again on the motorcycle in reverse order, with Shaun steering (wearing the tortoise like a helmet) and Wallace and Gromit on top.

Following the success of Wallace and Gromit's *Cracking Contraptions* on the Internet and on TV, Aardman decided that it was about time that the two of them started appearing in some adverts closer to home. As the chances of Putchin

Wallace's Inventions: the Car Tester

As a well-known inventor, Wallace is often called in to provide designs for commercial companies. Strangely, he's not often called back. Still, the Car Tester was one of his greatest triumphs – a rolling road on which a car could be placed and various weather effects like rain and wind simulated without the bother of having to get out into the great British countryside. Which, considering the trouble that Wallace got into with a motorcycle, a sidecar and a flock of sheep, is probably just as well.

pudding appearing in Britain was slim at best, the decision was made to go with Renault, who were launching their new Kangoo car and were looking for a stylish and yet appealing idea to match the stylish and yet appealing lines of the car. A commercial was put together based on *Cracking Contraptions*, with Wallace using one of his highly complex inventions to test the Kangoo before its release. The commercial starts with what looks like Wallace starting a 'Wallaced-up' version of the Kangoo and driving it along a country road with Gromit caught on the windscreen. Wallace tests the headlights and the windscreen wipers, twanging Gromit's nose in the process, but when the wind rushing past the car blows Gromit off we realize that the whole thing is on a rolling road like a conveyor belt, somewhere in Wallace's basement. Suddenly a piston shoots the car upwards on a platform, and it emerges *Thunderbirds*-style into the garden. The commercial went out across Europe on TV, although it only got a showing in the UK in cinemas.

More recently, Wallace and Gromit have begun to promote Jacob's Cream Crackers. Wallace's fondness for what looks remarkably like the aforementioned crackers is obvious right back in *A Grand Day Out*, where he risks life and limb to retrieve an armful of them while the rocket's fuse is burning away. In the new advert he is using another one of his Cracking Contraptions to test out various toppings on the crackers, but the machine blows up spectacularly, showering him and Gromit with crumbs. 'It's Apocalypse Chow!' he cries.

Above: Good thing nobody was using the pool. Opposite: Testing biscuit toppings? Wallace must be crackers! But it's worth the total devastation of the living room just to find that elusive perfect cracker topping.

The World of Wallace & Gromit

'Gromit makes a smashing camel'
Wallace & Gromit Alive on Stage in A Grand Night Out

In live-action film or television, it's entirely possible to have short scenes set in different locations: car parks, offices, shops and so on. All you have to do is find the right location and start filming. With Aardman's Wallace and Gromit TV films, however, all the sets have to be lovingly handcrafted from scratch. Large chunks of the action have to be set in these 'locations' in order to justify the effort of making them, which is one of the reasons why Wallace and Gromit always spend a lot of time at home. Interestingly, theatre is the same: you can't keep putting up and taking down scenery to create different places on the stage. And if you think about it that way, a stage version of Wallace and Gromit's adventures makes a lot more sense.

Wallace and Gromit Alive on Stage in A Grand Night Out burst upon an unsuspecting world in 1997, the brainchild of mime artist Andrew Dawson. It wasn't Dawson's first foray into representing television characters on stage: he and colleague Gavin Robertson had previously put together a theatrical version of Gerry Anderson's *Thunderbirds* in which they played not only the wooden puppets but also the Thunderbirds vehicles and various collapsing landmarks as well. The *Thunderbirds* play was first put on as what was effectively a cheap skit, but went on for six West End Seasons and had toured round the world several times (including, bizarrely, three visits to China).

Among other work, Andrew Dawson also teaches physical theatre around the country. It was this teaching that first brought him into contact with Aardman Animations.

Opposite: The cast of Wallace & Gromit in A Grand Night Out with Andrew Dawson.

Plot

Wallace is on the stage of the local playhouse, preparing an invited audience for the public unveiling of his latest invention: the Mark 1 Pantheatricon. It's a fully automated theatre 'with added add-ons', housed in a caravan. Wallace

tells the audience that he invented it after he joined WWADS – the West Wallaby Amateur Dramatics Society. It contains, somewhere within its high-tech circuitry, a brainwave activator that relays an entire role to an actor through a headset that they have to wear, meaning that they never forget a line! It also has a Theme Generator, which can switch themes from Musical to Western to Thriller at the drop of a hat, and a Costumerama, allowing instant generation of the appropriate costume for whatever theme has been chosen.

Aided by Gromit and Shaun the Sheep, Wallace begins his demonstration. At the press of a button the entire caravan unfolds itself onto the stage, providing an acting area, a back-stage area and a place for the musicians to sit.

Wallace is, however, put off his stride when Wendolene Ramsbottom turns up in the middle of his demonstration. She tells him that she wants to be friends again following their falling out over the matter of Preston the Robot dog and the sheep-rustling. She has bought a large box with her, and a newspaper which contains a startling story about the escape of penguin villain 'Feathers' McGraw from Fishhaven jail. He has, according to the newspaper report, sworn revenge on the pair who brought him to justice. That pair, Wallace realizes, are him and Gromit!

Above: Wallace (Paul Filipiak) and Gromit (Russ Edwards) act up behind Wendolene (Joyce Henderson).

As the demonstration of the Mark 1 Pantheatricon continues, Gromit is 'persuaded' to try out the Costumerama function. Aiming for a set of cowboy clothes, he emerges dressed as ballet dancer and is forced to perform Tchaikovsky's *Dance of the Sugar Plum Fairy* in front of everyone. Moments later the Costumerama forces him into opera garb, cowboy clothes, burlesque and folk dancing costumes. There's obviously been a malfunction.

Wallace, Wendolene and Gromit go round the back of the caravan to fix the Pantheatricon. While they are gone, Wendolene's abandoned box opens up and 'Feathers' McGraw steps out! It appears that the amoral avian has hypnotized Wendolene into acting as his assistant in a bizarre plan to get his revenge on Wallace and Gromit.

While 'Feathers' McGraw hides somewhere backstage, Wallace returns to the front of the auditorium with Wendolene and tells the audience that everything is now ready for a complete run-through of a theatrical production using the incomparable resources of the Mark 1 Pantheatricon. Although normally reluctant to appear on stage, Wendolene says she will join in (although we know that she's under the control of 'Feathers' McGraw).

Wallace sets about choosing a book as the basis for their experimental theatrical extravaganza. He decides against *The Silence of the Lambs* – probably wisely – and chooses instead a classic Victorian mystery in the style of Arthur Conan Doyle. The book is inserted into a slot in the Pantheatricon, and its

The World of Wallace & Gromit

plot and characters are analysed and dramatized. The costumerama springs into action, kitting Wallace out as a deerstalker-clad detective and Gromit as his indefatigable assistant. Shaun's responsibility is the provision of sound effects, but he keeps getting them wrong, forcing Wallace and Gromit to improvise.

Wallace and Gromit journey from their digs at Baker Street to Wensleydale Moor to aid Lady Wensleydale, whose husband has disappeared and whose cheese has come out stained red, as if with blood! The entire production is thrown into momentary confusion when Wendolene's penguin-induced hypnotic trance wears off and she realizes that she can't continue in her role as the local barmaid. Gromit takes over, but then discovers that he can't play the detective's assistant and the barmaid at the same time, so Shaun the Sheep takes over as the barmaid. 'Feathers' McGraw is forced to emerge from his hidey-hole and re-hypnotize Wendolene so that she can continue acting on the stage, where she keeps trying, and failing, to kill Wallace on the penguin's behalf.

In the play, the detective and his assistant make their way across the moors to Wensleydale Hall. Shaun reappears as the butler – Lambsbottom – but Feathers McGraw replaces the sheep and tries to poison the two heroes! They go to their rooms, where they intend getting a good night's sleep before attempting to solve the mystery of the disappearing Lord Wensleydale, but a hypnotized Wendolene tries once more to kill them while they pretend to be asleep.

> 'Alas, poor Yorick, I knew him well,
> A fellow of infinite jest
> He had a rather peculiar smell
> He kept hamsters under his vest.'

During a dramatic night-time chase scene through Wensleydale Manor, in which the detective and his assistant are following a mysterious hooded figure, the penguin uses a remote control to keep altering the theatrical style that the Mark 1 Pantheatricon is imposing upon the stagebound action. Wallace and Gromit just think that the machine is malfunctioning, as Wallace's machines are wont to do.

The chase finishes with the mysterious hooded figure (actually, Wendolene in her role as Lady Wensleydale) escaping through a hidden door in the library. Our detective and his assistant (actually, Wallace and Gromit) follow her to the moor, where Wendolene and Wallace break out of their roles and share a romantic moment alone.

Feathers McGraw arrives on stage, dressed as the detective's assistant. It's time to put his evil plan into action! He hits Wendolene with a stone, knocking her down. Wallace, seeing what he supposes to be Gromit striking down the woman he loves, fires Gromit from the play.

Wendolene, under the penguin's control, persuades Wallace to switch the Mark 1 Pantheatricon's theme to 'Cops and Robbers'. Using Wallace and the play as cover, Feathers McGraw and Wendolene start taking valuables from audience, who are supposed to think that this is all part of the action, Wallace realizes that something's afoot. During a confused finale, in which the Pantheatricon keeps switching themes, Wallace confronts the penguin, who attempts to kill him in a kebab slicing machine, but Gromit arrives just in time to rescue his master. A chase ensues, as it almost always does, and the penguin's schemes are undone when his own bomb explodes near him, blowing him back to prison again.

Wallace apologizes to the audience for the chaos on stage, and Wendolene – recovered now from her hypnosis – resumes her bittersweet romance with Wallace.

Behind the scenes

Andrew Dawson's connections with Aardman go back further than *Wallace and Gromit Alive on Stage in A Grand Night Out*. As a fully fledged mime artist (or, rather, a practitioner of 'physical theatre') he had been bought in to advise the animators at Aardman on how their creations should move.

'I did some workshops before the animators even got to Aardman,' Andrew remembers. 'What's funny is they do use their own body movements – their own idiosyncrasies come out in the puppets, in the animation – but it's interesting to make them more aware of themselves in order that they can provide a common element of movement in the animation. And of course now, on the more recent Wallace and Gromit films, and on *Chicken Run*, more than one animator is animating one figure. It's not just Nick fiddling around in his back room with Wallace. So, in a way, we have to agree what the style is.'

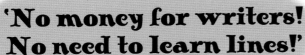

'No money for writers! No need to learn lines!'

Having been aware of Wallace and Gromit for some time, Andrew Dawson's realization that they could be translated to the stage came as something of a bolt from the blue.

'It was my son,' he reveals. 'My son was watching one of the videos. And although I had seen it many times, I suddenly looked at it slightly differently and thought, "Well, d'you know, I wonder if you could just put that on stage? What would it be like if Wallace walked around as a person? We made puppets walk around: why not do another animation?" So I contacted David Sproxton at Aardman – he'd been a big fan of *Thunderbirds* and had followed our work over the years, so I'd known him for a long time, on and off. I said, "How about it?" and he said, "If anyone ought to do it, you should."'

Unlike the TV version of Wallace and Gromit, where Nick Park started out with a set of images which were then connected together by a script, Andrew approached the project more traditionally.

'I think I wrote the script first and then we did some short workshops with some friends. And we fiddled around with visually how little you needed to make a Wallace and Gromit.'

As with *Thunderbirds*, Andrew was surprised how easy it was to recreate the characters in a different form.

'In a way it's easier to take something non-human,' he says, 'like plasticine figures or puppets and put them on stage, than it is to take something familiar, that is already made of people ... I instinctively knew from *Thunderbirds* that the reason it worked was the twinkle in our eye. The joke was with *us*, not with the fact that it was on stage; it was the fact that we were going "Look at what we're doing!" In a way, we needed to capture that with Wallace and Gromit as well.'

Although the workshopped version of *Wallace and Gromit Alive on Stage in A Grand Night Out* actually made it to a live stage show, Andrew was dissatisfied.

'I always remember,' he laughs, 'that the opening was absolutely fantastic, but once you got stuck into this story it just became very complicated with five characters, and trying to figure out who was going where and when. And everybody had props! Endless props! For me, props were an absolute nightmare! "Where's my notepad?" "I don't care about your notepad, just pretend you've got one!" "No we have to actually have one!"'

To help pull the show into a more coherent form, writer Bob Baker was brought in to overhaul the script. Bob had previously worked with Nick Park on *The Wrong Trousers* and *A Close Shave*, and also wrote some early drafts of the first Wallace and Gromit movie, *Wallace & Gromit Curse of the WereRabbit*. He was, as much as anyone, an expert on how to write for the two characters.

'I don't have a history of scriptwriting,' Andrew Dawson admits freely. 'I mean, I can invent shows, but writing scripts is another thing. Bob came in, made various changes and beefed it up a bit.'

'I went to see it at Crawley,' Bob Baker remembers, 'and then I saw it again somewhere else. I looked at it and I said, "Well, there's a lot of things that Wallace and Gromit have done, but there's no story." I said I would rewrite it in return for a credit and part of the action, and I actually rewrote it in about four days.'

The key to the success of the stage show was the fact that the audience had to believe that they were really seeing Wallace and Gromit on stage. That meant translating two plasticine figures 6in or so high into human proportions, making them move properly and giving them those familiar characteristics and mannerisms.

'It was funny,' he says: 'the actor who played Wallace – Paul Filipiak – was like Wallace in real life. I hadn't realized when I was casting him. In rehearsals we used to say, "Okay, Paul, can we do this scene?" and he'd go, "Well, alright, if you like; what, now?"

"Yes, *now* Paul." '

With the right actor cast and the right walk and mannerisms developed, the rest was just suggestion. Unusually, Andrew Dawson decided to focus on getting Wallace's nose right.

'He just had a little button nose,' he states. 'They all had noses, all the characters, because traditionally a clown's nose is a fantastic disguise. A nose is like a mask: you can just put a nose on and somebody's expression will completely change. So we just gave him a little nose – he had very short hair, and he was very tall, and this little nose was enough, with that over-knitted sweater.'

Gromit was equally simple, considering he was a dog.

'If you're going to evoke their characters then you can't have that much around the eyes, so we messed around a lot with what would make a good muzzle ... I remember we spent a lot of time thinking about electronic ears – remote control ears. It would have been a nightmare: you know they'll break ...'

In the end, rather than go for fully animatronic, radio-controlled ears, Andrew Dawson went for a low-tech solution.

'They're just made from coat hangers,' he laughs. 'Metal coat hangers. The actor basically wears a baseball cap that's strapped under his chin. You can pull the ears down, and you can push them up, and they just stay in their positions. You can literally bend them in any way you like. And, of course, the

The World of Wallace & Gromit

BALLET

Above: Gromit (Russ Edwards) shows what a multi-talented dog he is.

joke was that you forgave the actor the actual action of doing it.'

Not surprisingly, Wallace's object of affection in the play is Wendolene, former owner of the local wool shop and unconvicted sheep rustler. Creating a convincing Wendolene was even simpler than Wallace and Gromit.

As Andrew says: 'Wendolene just had a kind of bicycle helmet, but in the shape of her hair. And a nose. And some very nice, slightly oversized pearls.'

The show was designed to provide audiences with something immediately familiar, to get them used to the idea of seeing Wallace and Gromit on stage. What Andrew Dawson did, effectively, was to recreate the beginning of *A Grand Day Out* and use that as a springboard for the rest of the play.

'It opens with an empty stage,' he remembers. 'You think you're seeing the back wall of the theatre, but you're not. And there's a big staircase, so it's Wallace's cellar. Wallace walks down the stairs into the cellar, and he starts to draw something. Eventually he comes in front of the curtain and tells the audience that he'd had enough of the film business and that he thought he ought to tread the boards for a bit, so he's been designing a Pantheatricon, which is his ultimate theatre machine. And then the curtain goes up, and you get the Pantheatricon revealed on stage – it's a whopping great caravan, but it looks like *A Grand Day Out*'s rocket. It opens, and a stage slides out, and the roof comes off, and it's got lights in it, and a moving backdrop.'

Writer Bob Baker still remembers the stage show with fondness, tinged perhaps with a touch of regret for what it might have been.

'We did a few shows outside of London,' he recalls. 'Cardiff, and the Bristol Old Vic, and then we went into London for the Christmas run, which was very successful.'

Audiences loved the show, but for Andrew Dawson there was one person in particular whose approval was vitally important – Nick Park. Fortunately, Nick wasn't appalled by what had been done to his favourite creations.

'Oh, he loved it,' Andrew recalls. 'I think he particularly loved the opening, because it was just so *A Grand Day Out*, and he just saw his whole history right in front of his eyes. People [accepted] the characters, you know: the audiences went, "Oh yeah, there's Wallace and Gromit," and they didn't bat an eyelid. I knew instinctively from *Thunderbirds* that they would, but I think for Nick it must have been very weird.'

In fact, it was. Recalling the stage show now, Nick Park says: 'What was most surreal about it was when the curtain opened for the first time, and there was Wallace's cellar, and Wallace came walking down the cellar stairs, and he sat at the table and started drawing. It was just like the opening of the cellar scene in *A Grand Day Out*. It was uncanny. I had a lot of respect for that company,' he says, 'and for Andrew Dawson. It couldn't have been in better hands.'

'The penguin is mightier than the sword'

Wallace & Gromit take on Project Zoo

From their original base on television, Wallace and Gromit have expanded their amazing adventures in all directions. As well as comics, books and the theatre, they've even managed to take the odd excursion onto our computer screens.

It was winter 2003 when the plasticine pair took full advantage of computer technology, bursting into the shops in a game called *Project Zoo*. This was an entirely new adventure for them, following directly on from the events of *The Wrong Trousers*. The game allows you to take control of Gromit, advised, of course, by the ever-present Wallace, in an investigation of strange goings-on in their local zoo. The game contains six different environments, 24 missions and 12 sub-levels, along with a whole raft of treats and rewards, so there's plenty to keep the agile player busy.

'The computer game was one that was always pushed back in the nineties,' explains Sean Clarke, Aardman's Head of Marketing and Licensing. 'Because it was deemed that we work in plasticine, why would we do it in CGI [computer-generated imagery]? But then, I think, we tried to take a different approach by working with a developer *first* to get a feel that Nick was comfortable with, to try and replicate in CGI the whole tactile, plasticine look.'

Lucy Wendover, who works in Aardman's Marketing and Licensing department, is enthusiastic about *Project Zoo*. 'It's brand new material, it's got new characters, and Gromit is the hero in it!' she says. 'He just takes on this amazing superhero status! And it makes sense, because really he is the brains behind it all.'

'This is a fine how-do-you-do for the books!'

Plot

Wallace and Gromit have adopted a baby polar bear called Archie in the local zoo (the same zoo that the evil penguin 'Feathers' McGraw is incarcerated in, but we'll come to that later). One day they realize that it's Archie's birthday

so they head off to the zoo with a fish as a present to give to him. When they get there the zoo is locked up – it's the middle of the day, and neither of them understand what's happening. As they're trying to phone directory enquiries to find out what's happened to the zoo, a truck comes around the corner, and Gromit, ever the detective, spots the silhouette of evil penguin thief 'Feathers' McGraw driving. They also see Archie trapped in the cab of the truck, and realize pretty quickly that something's amiss.

Returning to West Wallaby Street, Wallace and Gromit build a giant Trojan penguin out of wood (as they would). Unsurprisingly, the inside of it looks exactly like their living room. Off they trundle, down the street, inside the Trojan Penguin, and when it arrives at the zoo gate Feathers spots it. Intrigued, his immediate reaction is that the object is a tribute to his greatness, and so he lets it in.

As soon as the Trojan Penguin is inside the zoo gates, Wallace and Gromit pop out and try to ambush the penguin, but he's way ahead of them. A chase ensues through various levels of 'Feathers's under-zoo base.

As Wallace and Gromit progress through the various levels, they gradually realize more and more what the penguin is doing. By the time they reach the final level they realize that he's kidnapped all the baby animals in the zoo in order to force their parents to do his bidding. The animals are working for him in every level of the massive base, using his Diamond O'Matic machine to create diamonds out of crushed ice and coal. The reason he wants diamonds is because they remind him of the ice at home, but it's up to Wallace and Gromit to stop him using whatever skills they possess – and a banana gun!

Wallace & Gromit take on Project Zoo

Left: Gromit heroically crosses dangerous bridges and grabs floating nuts in order to help Wallace build new inventions in the computer game.
Opposite: The new Wallace and Gromit computer game, Project Zoo.

Behind the scenes

Aardman decided that the time was right for a Wallace and Gromit computer game. 'We went looking for a like-minded developer,' says Helen Neno, Aardman's licensing manager. 'Frontier came up with a great concept, which felt like it belonged to Wallace and Gromit's world. It also helped that David Braben and his team at Frontier are real Wallace and Gromit fans, and understood what they would and wouldn't do. For instance, there are certain game genres that wouldn't have been right.'

Frontier were already well established and well respected as creators of computer games, but to help meet a complex delivery schedule a separate company – Bam Entertainment – were bought in to project manage the game's development.

'Aardman worked very closely with Frontier and Bam to get the right look and feel for the game,' says Rachael Carpenter, Aardman's Product Development Manager. 'Nick was involved in the whole process, as much as his time allowed. He had very clear ideas from the start – whilst the in-game characters are obviously computer generated, he still wanted them to have a plasticine look and feel. He also wanted the characters to behave as they did in the films. One of the first obstacles to overcome was how to conquer the in-game enemies without actually killing them. Frontier developed a series of hilarious and non-lethal weapons such as the turnip-launcher which enabled players to stun, but not kill, the various animals who are out to hinder Wallace and Gromit's progress. We were fortunate in getting time with some

'The zoo's gone ex-directory? This is most irregular!'

The World of Wallace & Gromit

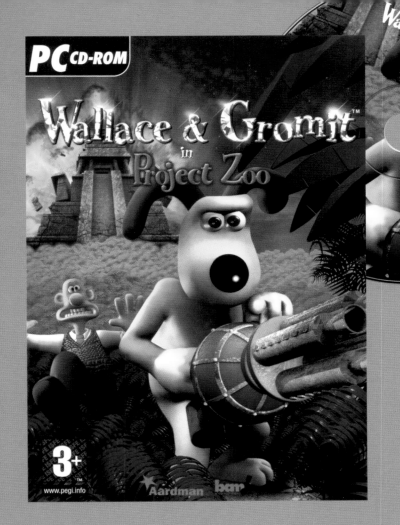

of our animators, who worked with Frontier to try and get the characters moving as they should. We also supplied Frontier with replacement mouths for Wallace, exactly the same as the animators at the studio use, to show the different sounds and to synchronise lip movements with the words.'

There were, however, still some compromises that had to be made in getting Wallace and Gromit into a computer game format.

'Nick was clear that Gromit could obviously never die!' Rachael adds. 'So we had to come up with a solution which would still present a challenge to the game player but wouldn't upset anyone concerned for Gromit's welfare. Frontier developed a health indicator, which is a cheese and crackers icon on the screen: the more that Gromit gets injured, the more the crackers appear to vanish. You can collect more throughout the game, but if they disappear altogether the worst that happens is that you have to start all over again from the point where you last saved.'

This game seemed to lend itself well to moving a character around and solving puzzles,' explains Marcus Fielding, BAM's Head of Development. 'You have the start, middle and end of a storyline, you have the environments – you have ice, you have snow – you have five big levels – it lends itself well to that.'

One of Nick Park's key concerns was with the movement and the look of the characters, as Marcus recalls.

'He was involved right at the beginning with the concept. From there on the meetings progressed to showing him animations of Gromit, starting out with four legs. Then he bought into the idea of putting him on two legs, and that opened up a whole new world of different moves: jumps, twirls, whatever.'

'We decided early on that you should play as Gromit,' chips in Aardman's Rachael Carpenter. 'After all, he is the real hero of the duo. However, at first it was a struggle trying to make him be as acrobatic as he needs to be whilst he is on four paws. Frontier did some early development to show us how Gromit could move if he was up on two feet, which convinced Nick that it could work. The compromise was that at certain points in the game Wallace whistles for Gromit and then puts him on a lead. This, and the fact that when he swims during the game it is, in fact, doggie paddle, reminds us that whilst he might be a hero he is still Wallace's faithful dog.'

During his perilous and time-consuming exertions, Gromit finds time to visit the toilet for a few moments during one game level.

'Nick injected a stroke of genius into the script,' Marcus readily admits. 'His input really was in the detail. "Wallace wouldn't wave his arms so rapidly, he would slow them down," – and that was the kind of input we needed. He was open to ideas; open for us to explore karate moves, jumping backwards, things that we never thought we could do at the beginning.'

'They've been very good at wanting feedback, and taking on comments,' Nick Park says of Frontier. They were interested in what we thought all the time. We've had animators go there and comment on all the movements, trying to get it as close as possible.'

Of course, the 'look' of the characters was only half the battle. Just as important was the way Wallace sounded. Actor Peter Sallis has been providing the voice for the Northern inventor since the very first TV film, and it's almost impossible to imagine Wallace with someone else's voice. All of Peter Sallis's lines as Wallace in the game were scripted for him by writer Tristan Davies (in conjunction with an Aardman script editor). In total he gets something like 7,000 words of dialogue in *Project Zoo* which, ironically, might be the most the actor has ever had to say as Wallace. To be fair, though, most of the lines are short phrases such as: 'Cut that out!', but there are a couple of real belters in there. In fact, Wallace gets so many lines in *Project Zoo* that Aardman's co-founder David Sproxton directed Peter's voice recording over three separate sessions in London. It was a key element.

Stop-motion animation is a slow process. Everyone knows that. Those little plasticine figures have to be painstakingly moved, a little bit at a time, and individual frames of film exposed to give the impression of smooth movement. On average, the animators at Aardman manage to produce something in the region of four to six seconds of usable film per day. One might imagine that the production of a computer game was considerably faster than this, but in fact it takes an awfully long time to get a game like *Project Zoo* finished to everyone's satisfaction.

At one point in the game Wallace and Gromit end up at Red Leicester Square station (named following an internal competition within Aardman to name a station).

'I think two and a half years is a realistic figure,' Marcus Fielding reveals. 'You could say it was more because there's a lot of technology that had to be developed before Nick would even say, "yes, you can go ahead with the animations", but two and a half years is about right for the actual game. It had a very large pre-production period where we experimented with the concepts, then we had about 12–16 months for production, where we produced the game design documents and the technical design documents and made the game.'

Once the game was finished, it had to go through an exhaustive testing process to ensure that it was hard enough to hold the interest of a range of players but not too hard to put them off. The game has been designed so that it would

The World of Wallace & Gromit

Right: Wallace and Gromit fly through a volcanic environment (beneath West Wallaby Street) in Wallace's autogyro.

take an average gamer at least ten hours to complete. Little rewards have been built in at various points. For instance, whenever you get through an entire level in the game you might be able to view an episode of *Wallace and Gromit's Cracking Contraptions*, clips from *The Wrong Trousers* or interviews with Nick Park, David Braben (the man in charge of game developers Frontier) and Tony Williams (Bam's Managing Director).

The game also contains rewards of a more subtle kind, for those discerning players who might whizz through the entire thing in less than the expected ten hours. Certain aspects of the game are subtle parodies of other well-known computer games, and might raise a small, knowing chuckle from the players ...

'I don't want anything just to be a money-making spin-off,' Nick Park insists. 'Anything we do should be good quality in itself. That's what we really wanted for the game. We've put a lot in, a lot of research and development. We wanted the environments to be rich and the humour to be good and original, so it feels creative. I think it's very largely achieved it.' He smiles. 'I play it myself,' he says sheepishly. 'It's really good.'

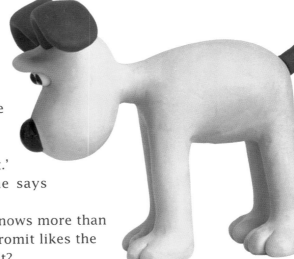

And, frankly, if the man who knows more than anyone else about Wallace and Gromit likes the game, it has to be good, doesn't it?

'An absurd chap, in the position of Cary Grant'
The music

People think of Wallace and Gromit as a self-contained duo, but there is a shadowy third presence always standing at their shoulders. His name is Julian Nott, and he wrote the music for all three films. That music – the sprightly brass band theme tune in particular – is as irreplaceable as Wallace's tank top or Gromit's occasional sidelong glances at the audience.

Julian was a student at the National Film and Television School at the same time that Nick Park was finishing off the first of the Wallace and Gromit films – *A Grand Day Out*. Needing a composer and chronically short of cash, Nick automatically thought about getting someone from the school to provide some music.

'He'd actually commissioned another composer,' Julian remembers, 'but that composer dropped out – he had other commitments – and I took over at the last minute. Nick didn't really get much of a chance to choose me – it just happened; I was there, and he needed somebody quick. In fact it was the Head of Animation at the film school at the time who suggested that I did it. To persuade me, he showed me the best eight gags from *A Grand Day Out*, one by one, so I didn't see the rest of the film until later!'

Like so many others before and since, Julian was charmed by Nick's skill and obvious talent.

'It was utterly fresh and new,' he says. 'In some ways the gags in *A Grand Day Out* are the best of the gags in the whole of Wallace and Gromit. I thought it was hilarious – I was very keen to work on it.'

Unlike some directors, Nick Park trusted Julian to come up with something suitable for the film, rather than interfering at every step.

'We went through the film together,' Julian explains, 'saying where there would be music and where there wouldn't – the normal system. With that film, and the others, there was very little time. It was all a bit of a rush because while I was doing the music, he was doing the sounds. There would be a rough sort of discussion, then I'd go away and do it, then he'd come and hear it, say what he liked and what he didn't like, and I would do again.'

There was one thing, however, that Nick was dead set on having.

'Nick had one big comment,' Julian recalls. 'Because it's all set somewhere ill-defined in the North of England, he thought it would be nice if we had music that people associate with that region – a brass band. The trouble was that, because there wasn't much money, we couldn't afford a brass band. I just went as close as I could. They aren't actually brass band instruments at all, they're orchestral brass instruments, but they do make quite a fat noise. And he's right, it works.'

The increasing scale of the three films meant that Julian had more resources to play with as time went on, although not much more time.

'With *The Wrong Trousers* and *A Close Shave* the music is played by an

The World of Wallace & Gromit

Opposite: Gromit considered that Wallace's conker-playing device was a little too... medieval... for its own good.

orchestra,' he says. 'In *A Grand Day Out* there is a very small orchestra – about fifteen people – and some of it I played myself on some very nasty, cheap late, 1980s synthesisers which I can't bear to listen to now.'

Having studied film and TV composition as a serious academic subject, Julian is well aware how different the music for the three Wallace and Gromit films is from the majority of animated film music.

'A lot of animated films have very child-like music,' he points out: 'plinky-plonky music. Also they're scored from beginning to end – music everywhere. The approach we took was scoring it like a live action film, like a real drama with real actors. That's why there isn't music all the way through. It's a fairly adult approach.'

It's well known – and admitted by the man himself – that Nick Park was influenced by a whole series of other films when putting *The Wrong Trousers* and *A Close Shave* together. Similarly, although not to the same extent, Julian's music for the films makes little nods of acknowledgement in certain directions.

'I have done that,' he admits. 'Sometimes explicitly, sometimes other people see it where I don't. In *The Wrong Trousers* there are elements of Bernard Herrman's Hitchcock music, and that was deliberate. It's part of the comedy strategy of Wallace and Gromit to take particular genres and refer to, and treat them, with respect. At the same time you have a bit of plasticine, an absurd chap, in the position of Cary Grant.'

Julian Nott isn't particularly analytical about his undoubted composing skills. He doesn't pick apart what he is doing in the way that some other film composers do.

'What goes through my brain is completely unknown to me,' he says. 'It just sort of happens. My fingers work and out comes something, and why I don't know. When I do it, I don't think of influences at all. I don't think of any other music. I don't think there's any other music that *is* like Wallace and Gromit.'

This instinctive approach shows itself most particularly in the fact that Julian did not attempt to impose any particular coherence on the three films – any repeated themes, or *leitmotifs*. He just let the music flow.

"I saw each film as an individual. I really didn't refer back to the ones before. However, I am the same person and if there's unity it comes from that."

Even now, a year or so before the new Aardman movie *Wallace & Gromit Curse of the WereRabbit* is planned for release, he is already working on the music in association, of course, with Nick Park. And he still looks back at what he accomplished

'I would do *A Grand Day Out* differently now, in that I wouldn't use the synthesisers I had to use. But what gives them their character is all the constraints that were placed on them at the time. They are what they are, and they shouldn't be changed.'

The music

'Don't forget, you can't write charm'
Getting the voices right

In the same way that the merest glimpse of Wallace's enormously wide mouth, toothy grin and strangely flat head are enough to render him instantly recognizable, just one or two words in that mellifluous Northern accent are sufficient for him to be identified without any possibility of mistake. Nobody speaks like Wallace (although, of course, with one or two exceptions, nobody else in the entirety of *A Grand Day Out*, *The Wrong Trousers*, *A Close Shave* and *Wallace and Gromit's Cracking Contraptions* apart from Wallace speaks at all). He is vocally, as in every other way, one of a kind.

It's undeniably the talent and creative energy of Nick Park that has propelled Wallace and Gromit to the stratospheric popularity they currently enjoy, but it's arguable that Wallace's distinctive voice has played its own small part. Back when Nick was first putting together *A Grand Day Out*, while he was still a student, the voice he heard in his head whenever he thought about Wallace was the voice of a particular actor called Peter Sallis, and so, with the naivety of youth, Nick approached him and asked if he would contribute his vocal talents to what was effectively a student film. And Peter Sallis said yes.

'I really never had anyone else in mind,' Nick says. 'Being a student at the time, I couldn't really afford an actor of his calibre, but he was the first person I thought of. We got in contact with him, and he came to the film school and recorded. I think we managed to pay him £50, or something like that. I think he was probably doing it as a favour for a student.'

Born in 1921, Peter Sallis has performed on film, stage and TV for some forty-six years. On TV he has played parts as diverse as a British Secret Service agent in *The Avengers* (1964) and a renegade scientist in a future ice-age in *Doctor Who* (1967). On stage he has acted alongside Ralph Richardson, Edith Evans, Laurence Olivier, Judy Dench, John Gielgud and Orson Welles – perfect preparation for working with a plasticine dog, one might think.

'I've seen him in old films,' Nick Park points out enthusiastically: '*Legend of the Werewolf* [1974], where he plays the chief policeman or something, and *Taste The Blood of Dracula!* [1970].'

Despite his near ubiquity in 1960s and '70s film and TV, it is his long-running performance as the sardonic Norman Clegg in the BBC's hit comedy *Last of the*

Opposite: Just how lazy is a man who makes machines to play games for him?

PUTTING FOR BEGINNERS

Above: What bait do you use to catch catfish? Fish?

Summer Wine that has bought him national fame. He first played the part of Clegg in 1973, and was still going strong decades later in 2003, having appeared in something like 225 episodes. It was, of course, his regular appearances in that series that led to Nick Park thinking of him as the voice of Wallace.

'Wallace was automatically Peter Sallis,' he says, 'especially because I thought he was Northern! The mild mannered Northern-ness of his character, in *Last of the Summer Wine*, particularly spoke to me. I sent him a script and he recorded it on his own home tape recorder and sent me back a cassette – "Is this what you're looking for?" kind of thing. On that tape, I realized that he wasn't Northern! He was more like a newsreader! That shocked me.'

For something that started out as a role in a short animated student film, Peter Sallis's portrayal of Wallace has continued for almost as long as his portrayal of Norman Clegg.

'It's funny,' Nick says, 'because I first worked with him over 20 years ago. Because it took me so long to make *A Grand Day Out*, I recorded him at the beginning and did all the lip-synch animation and everything, then I needed to do some pick-ups at the end. Peter has this story that he recorded this thing, forgot about it, did many more episodes of *Last of the Summer Wine*, then one day got a phone call from me saying, "I've finished!" He had to stop and think, who was this? And what has he finished?'

Peter Sallis's portrayal of Wallace has also branched out beyond the TV films,

The World of Wallace & Gromit

into a medium that didn't even exist when he first vocalised those flat Northern vowels – the computer game. He recently provided something like 7,000 words of dialogue for *Wallace and Gromit in 'Project Zoo'* – which is more than he had in the three TV films plus *Cracking Contraptions*.

'To me, he *is* Wallace,' Nick Park admits. 'No-one else could quite do it the same really. He brings such a quality to it. It's been a combination that's worked really well. Peter put his finger on it when we were talking about the writing of this new film: he said, "Don't forget, you can't write charm." I thought, that's true. It's quite flattering – what he's saying is there's a charm that happens, that you don't need Hollywood writers and stuff like that.'

> 'To me, he IS Wallace. No-one else could quite do it the same really. He brings such a quality to it.'
> Nick Park

Nick is obviously deeply grateful to Peter Sallis for his ongoing contributions to the success of the character, but Peter has a soft spot for Wallace and for Nick as well. He must have, otherwise he wouldn't have kept coming back to play him.

'I went to dinner with him recently,' says Nick, 'and we were just joking about things in general. He said it actually made him so happy to have got this part, especially later on in life. He said, "I would rather have had this than a full-time job at the National Theatre."'

Peter has kept largely silent about the part of Wallace. But then again, he is a reticent man who has said little about his acting career as a whole. He has, however, let one or two things slip over the years.

'I can't pretend that I brought anything to it that was very unusual,' he says reflectively, 'except that it sounds like Wallace *ought* to make a noise like that. "Smashing toast, Gromit!"'

Getting the voices right

'Where are Wallace & Gromit?'
A close shave in New York

Wallace and Gromit are in the fortunate position of having an experienced publicist named Arthur Sheriff who has succeeded in making them a household name. Arthur first bumped into David Sproxton and Peter Lord shortly after Nick Park had finally finished *A Grand Day Out*.

'I was looking after the British Animation festival,' Arthur explains, 'which was held in Bristol. It was 1989, and I went down there for the duration of the festival and met Peter Lord and David Sproxton, and it was then that they told me that they were putting *Creature Comforts* [the short film that Nick had completed for Aardman in which the words of ordinary members of the public were put into the plasticine mouths of animals in a zoo] and *A Grand Day Out* in for the Oscars. They knew how to enter the films, but they didn't know how to back them up in any way should they be lucky enough to win. I had a public relations company in London at the time, and I made a deal with Aardman that I would look after them for a while. We negotiated the tiniest fee you can imagine, and I said that I'd do it for six months. If we made any progress, we could decide whether this was an ongoing situation. There were only 16 of them at the time. Marketing and PR was just not on the agenda.'

The big irony was that Aardman had entered both *Creature Comforts* and *A Grand Day Out* for the Animation section of the Academy of Motion Picture Arts and Sciences Awards, meaning that Nick Park was effectively in competition with himself, given that he had animated both films.

'*Creature Comforts* won,' Arthur recalls. '*A Grand Day Out* was overshadowed by *Creature Comforts* for the next year or so, but even when Nick won the Oscar the whole thing was so hard to get into newspapers. They really didn't want to know. Animation was this lowly category in the Oscars – kind of in the arts and crafts section. Newspapers just wouldn't write about it. My challenge obviously was to turn that around.'

Opposite: Wallace,
Wendolene, Gromit and
Shaun sing Christmas
carols while a mysterious
figure watches from behind.

Arthur Sheriff quickly realized that publicizing plasticine was going to be something of an uphill struggle.

'Strangely enough the broadsheets came in first,' he says. 'I would consider myself lucky if, in a Saturday review section, I got a picture and a caption. The key that opens the door to all the wonderful reviews, as I soon found out – and it sounds so obvious – is to get people to see it. A lot of people had heard of *Creature Comforts*, but it wasn't particularly fashionable to be watching animation then. Animation was still *Snow White* and *Mickey Mouse* and whatever. In the early nineties it started to change, and of course Nick was on that wave.'

Despite the success that Wallace and Gromit have enjoyed in the past ten years, that first showing of *A Grand Day Out* might easily have been their last. What little press attention came Aardman's way was directed somewhere else.

'*A Grand Day Out* suffered somewhat through the originality of *Creature Comforts*,' Arthur admits. 'When you look at *A Grand Day Out* now, it's wonderful. It's beautiful. You love it so much because it's Nick's first work, and the introduction to Wallace and Gromit. But on the other hand, and I'm sure Nick wouldn't mind me saying this, it's slow! It takes a long time to get to the point. *A Grand Day Out* was extremely hard to promote.'

Channel 4, who had originally shown *A Grand Day Out*, had little interest in a follow-up. Over at the BBC, however, things were different.

'Colin Rose was there by now,' Arthur remembers. 'He had set up the Animation Unit and he was an integral part of this whole thing. In fact, it was Alan Yentob who commissioned *The Wrong Trousers*. He was head of all those wonderful strands at the time – arts programmes like *Arena*.'

As well as commissioning a new Wallace and Gromit film, the BBC also agreed to show the first one again. In the time between the two films, Aardman had gone from strength to strength.

'Time seemed to fly by from *A Grand Day Out* up until *The Wrong Trousers*,' Arthur Sheriff says. 'The studio was becoming active, expanding. The 16 people that I joined suddenly became 32, then 64.'

Despite the fact that he had originally only signed on as Aardman's publicist for a six-month stint, Arthur had realized two things. First, he was enjoying himself. Secondly, Aardman needed him.

'What I became extremely aware of was that the layout of a page in a newspaper can be influenced by how good a photograph is, and there were only three or four photographs from each film. People would ask me for more photographs, or different photographs. They were wanting to put in something that nobody else had seen. Aardman had never paid attention to this. It was a revelation to them that they had to take photographs of what they were actually filming. It's something that I instigated. Today it just sounds like common sense, but these guys were purely film makers and, to a certain degree, if the film was shown and people didn't like it that was fine. They weren't commercially driven at all, and still aren't.'

A close shave in New York

By the time of the first TV showing of *The Wrong Trousers*, Arthur had formulated a strategy to maximize the publicity. He knew that Aardman had produced an absolutely amazing programme; the trick was to make other people realize the same thing before it was shown.

'By this time,' he recalls, 'we were in the broadsheets and the midrange papers, but we were not going into the tabloids. The tabloids did not want to know us – we were much too highbrow for them. We were getting into the *Mail* and the *Express* alright, but when *The Wrong Trousers* came along for the first time we put together a whole PR and marketing plan. The plan on *The Wrong Trousers* was to present it as a West End movie in preview theatres – something virtually unheard of for a thirty-minute TV programme. We hired a preview theatre for two weeks, and at 6.30 and 8.30 every night we had previews. It was my job to get every journalist that I wanted to write about it to come along and see it. We succeeded very well. The pre-publicity for the first showing of *The Wrong Trousers* was absolutely outstanding, and it was all because of this plan.'

The Wrong Trousers won an Oscar – Nick Park's second – in March, 1995. Again, Arthur Sheriff was faced with the problem of a largely indifferent UK press. 'The trick,' he remembers, 'was for Nick to have a mobile phone with him – and this is in the days when mobile phones were like bricks. I remained in London to activate the media. Nick's success was not featured in the Oscar news as much as I felt it should be, until the *Today* programme on BBC Radio 4 spoke to him live from the post-Oscar party. I negotiated for weeks to get them to do it. It wasn't until that morning that they actually said yes. That was one of the major breaking points because *Today* sets the media agenda for the day. After that interview, the phone in the office lit up with all sorts of requests to talk to Nick, and then the publicity machine really started snowballing.'

It was, in hindsight, inevitable that the success of the second Wallace and Gromit TV film would lead to a third one being made, and Aardman quickly swung behind the production.

'We finished *A Close Shave* around about September, 1995,' Arthur says. 'All the executives at the BBC had seen it and were raving like you can't believe. In fact the story goes that BBC1 wanted to show it as the highlight of the Christmas festivities, but it was a BBC2 commission and BBC2 fought tooth and nail to keep it. How right they were – on Christmas Eve, when it was shown, it got the top viewing audience for the whole year for any BBC2 programme.'

Like its predecessor, *A Close Shave* walked away with the Oscar, for best short animation. It was an unprecedented event – a small British company beating the vast Disney corporation, plus all of their smaller rivals, with what was essentially a journey into a surreal world of sheep and inventions.

For Arthur, this is when the entire thing turned around, and rather than fighting to get stories into the press he was fighting to stop them. 'When Nick won the third Oscar, the world's media wanted to know. We started to turn down major publicity coups. By that time we'd also had big colour spreads in the *Sunday Times*, and the tabloids started to come in then. Nick got the CBE later that year, in the June Honours list, and he got front page coverage from the *Sun*.

Things exploded from there, and Nick was literally being asked to do everything from open supermarkets to you name it. In those days Nick only had to sneeze and it was in the papers. We had an offer from a tabloid for Wallace to edit the paper for a day. You have to keep yourself in check and say, "Hey, we're film makers, let's not run away with it."'

To capitalize on the publicity of the Oscars, Arthur Sheriff had arranged five days of intensive interviews for Nick Park in New York. Little did he know it, but the trip was to turn into a virtual public relations hurricane that would sweep the world, and the spark that lit the blue touchpaper was the fact that the trip involved Wallace and Gromit as well as Nick and Arthur. The models from *A Close Shave*, along with the motorcycle and sidecar combination, were packed into a large black box and carried to the USA so they could be used for publicity shots and to generate extra interest.

'We flew out on 21 October, a Saturday,' Arthur remembers. 'Nick and I flew out from Heathrow and the plane got stacked up over New York because a north-easterly gale had blown in and they'd had six months of rainfall in one afternoon. So our flight was delayed for three hours, circling around. Everything

Below: Painting Gromit's nose red to fit in with the festive season seems a little permanent ... and the red splashes on the snow will probably scare the postman come the morning.

is down in New York, trees are blocking roads, and by the time we get out of the plane and through the airport, the limousine that was meeting us had gone. So we got into a yellow cab. We get to our hotel, and as we draw up it is bucketing down like you cannot believe. We try to get out, and immediately there are ten people trying to get in. So there's confusion. The cabby doesn't get out because it's pouring with rain, I pay him and he opens the trunk from within, as you can do. The trunk opens, the hotel porter comes out, grabs our bags, runs in because it's pouring with rain and he doesn't want to get wet, and we assume he's got everything. Meanwhile, the cab has disappeared down 56th Street. We're in the hotel lobby, and Nick says, "Where are Wallace and Gromit?" I said, "You've got them." He said, "No, you've got them." Nick runs out of the hotel to try and spot the cab, and of course there's a sea of yellow cabs, you wouldn't know one from another.'

The World of Wallace & Gromit

'This was very serious,' explains Arthur, 'because they're the originals, and it's hard to put a price on them. If I was to sell the originals I could get hundreds of thousands of pounds for them. To physically make them again it's probably about £10,000. The motorbike and sidecar alone cost £4,000 or £5,000 to make.'

The first question was, how to get them back?

'Nick goes off to bed – he's quite upset. The next day we issue an All Points Bulletin, like they used to do on American TV cop series. We got Nick to do a sketch of Wallace and Gromit, with details of how we lost them, and we started to fax this to all the TV stations and radio stations and newspapers. We followed up on the phone, but I was getting a lot of rejections, so I call one of the local radio stations, and I say, "I represent *three-time Oscar winner* Nick Park …" "Hold the line!" The chief reporter comes on, and says, "Can we do an interview with you now?" That was when I realized how to crack it in America.'

Where the idiosyncrasy of two plasticine models going missing failed to attract any attention, the mention of Nick Park's Oscars did the trick. Suddenly, he was a celebrity, and everyone wanted a piece of him.

'CNN came round, filmed Nick, he described Wallace and Gromit, and they put it on every few minutes on Sunday morning. This went on up until 9 am, and we're working like hell. Then I think to myself, "It's such a shame that all this is happening in America and folks at home can't enjoy it!" I open up my phone book and start calling newsrooms, and the first paper was the *Daily Telegraph*. I call the newsroom, and I say, "Hi, it's Arthur Sheriff, we've lost Wallace and Gromit in New York! The whole of America is looking for them!" The news editor said, "Arthur, you'll never believe this, we're all sat around here at 2 pm and there's no stories. There's nothing happening today – you've cracked it for us. Stay there – we'll have a journalist round in five minutes." Lo and behold a journalist from the *Daily Telegraph* arrives with a photographer in five minutes. I'm thinking, this is interesting. I get Nick doing that interview, and I call the *Daily Mail*. Exactly the same reaction – they get a journalist round. So I go tabloid, I call the *Sun*: exactly the same. So I call all nine national newspapers, and they all came around! Everyone was saying, "This is great, but Arthur, is it a stunt?" I said, "I promise you it's not a stunt." I even took a call from an ITN news TV crew in a plane who had flown over from the UK – they're circling Manhattan and they're on the phone to me, and they've flown in specially. I knew we had cracked it then.'

A close shave in New York

And it wasn't just America and England – for whatever reason, be it a slow news day, the Oscar connection or the essential eccentricity of the story itself, the entire world seemed to take an interest.

'Forget alone the English-speaking countries like Australia – this story broke in India, China … It was on page 3 of *Le Monde*. It was one of those gifts that just fall into your hands. You could never have *manoeuvred* the whole publicity circus, or set the whole thing up.'

Fortunately, the story has a happy ending.

'During all this phone call mayhem the taxi driver arrives, and is shown up to my room. He's got the box with Wallace and Gromit inside. He'd heard it on the radio. Lovely adorable Indian man, didn't speak a lot of English. I had $500 in my pocket that I wanted to give him and he wouldn't take a penny.'

'I remember getting onto the plane at JFK after the five terrifically successful days in NY,' Arthur laughs. 'I remember we were sitting in our seats and I ordered a large drink. Then the captain comes on the intercom and says, "You'll be pleased to know we have Nick Park on board, and Wallace and Gromit are safely in the hold." The whole plane gives Nick a round of applause. It was fantastic.'

The World of Wallace & Gromit

'Liable to be swayed by a penguin'

Why do we love Wallace & Gromit so much?

Although their total 'screen life' is still less than two hours, Wallace and Gromit have permeated the national and international consciousness in a way that other characters, who might have stacked up days, weeks or years of TV time, have failed to do. What is it about the flexible friends that speaks so loudly to us? What is it that makes up their characters? What, for instance, makes Wallace, Wallace?

'I think Wallace is a sort of obsessive,' explains David Sproxton. 'I wouldn't say he's uncaring, but he's blind to the consequences of his actions, and probably somewhat frightened of his own emotions. Never quite manages to pull it off with the ladies. He's very introverted, doesn't engage a lot, very much lives in his own world and, in a way, is very naive.'

'There's something very British about him,' explains Aardman's Kieran Argo. 'Wallace has a passion for making these stupid things where the amount of energy that goes into them defeats the whole object, but there's something absolutely fantastical about the fact that he can build a rocket in his basement and get to the Moon, and end up having a fight with this oven! I mean, how surreal is that?'

Steve Box, who assisted Nick Park with the animation on *The Wrong Trousers* and *A Close Shave* has his own ideas about Wallace's character. 'Wallace to me is completely "feet first",' he says. 'He sees something and it's like his eyes are bigger than his belly. Even though he must be very clever, because he makes these ingenious inventions which require a lot of skill and a lot of thought, he doesn't think of the application. It may be a really clever machine, but the application is ridiculous. It's usually the sort of thing that you could do much easier without a machine. There's that contradiction in him: he's a fraction selfish, a little unthinking, but good hearted.'

'The thing with Wallace, of course, is he never learns anything!' exclaims writer Bob Baker, who worked with Nick Park on the scripts for the second and third TV films. 'Whatever happens, he'll never learn anything from it at all!'

'I think Wallace touches on the Heath Robinson in all of us,' says Andrew Dawson, who not only assists the animators at Aardman with their interpretations of Wallace's movements and brought Wallace and Gromit to the

stage. 'Basically he is a child with open eyes. Children just go: "Look, that's amazing", or "Look how red that wall is", and you go, "Oh, I've never actually seen it like that, I've never really noticed."'

One might think that Gromit, who never talks during the entirety of the adventures he shares with his master, would be the simpler of the two characters. In fact, he's by far the most complicated.

'The fact that Gromit doesn't speak is a great bonus,' says Steve Box, 'because he's a thinker. He's internalizing and working out all the problems, and covering Wallace's tracks half the time.'

'Gromit's clearly more intelligent, and more far seeing,' agrees David Sproxton. 'He's very long-suffering about Wallace's inventor tendencies: "Oh God, here we go, we're going to end up in trouble here!" Well-intentioned as Wallace is, he often can't see the trap he's going to run into.'

'Gromit has to put up with him,' continues Steve Box. 'It's funny: there are contradictions in all great characters, and Gromit's is that he is incredibly intelligent and thoughtful, and yet he's a dog! He can drive a car, but he can't live in his own house in peace, which is what he should do.'

'Gromit serves as a juxtaposition between us and Wallace,' explains Andrew Dawson. 'Because without him we don't have anybody to comment on Wallace. Gromit can be with us to say, "Look how ridiculous this situation is!" But still he's endlessly positive – any other dog would go and live somewhere else! But he doesn't, he stays!'

In fact, we're not captivated by Wallace and Gromit at all. They are what they are – plasticine, cleverly animated. It's the relationship between them that captivates us. The bonds that connect them almost get stretched to breaking point by Wallace's thoughtless actions, and yet always pull them back together again.

'You can understand the relationship between Wallace and Gromit quite quickly,' says Kieran Argo: 'Gromit being the brains, Wallace being very enthusiastic – but there is something just fantastic about the characterization.'

'They're inseparable,' Steve Box adds, 'and all the films rely on the fact that they must stay together as a couple. They might be slightly wary, or they might be falling out, but they have to stick together. I think *The Wrong Trousers* is the ultimate piece so far, because their relationship is taken right to the wire.'

'I think it's a very British thing,' says Bob Baker, who did much to build that relationship into *The Wrong Trousers* and *A Close Shave*. 'It's a loyalty thing, where there's an expectation of loyalty from one to the other, but the lovely thing is that the totally honourable character is Gromit and the fickle one is Wallace. He has frailties, and is liable to be swayed by a penguin, or by an argument. So you've got this crazy situation where there's one who is totally loyal and another one

Opposite: Gromit is not pleased to see how much Shaun appreciates his cooking.

who's just a bit... stupid... but because of that, the other one loves him and the relationship stays stable. Gromit can forgive, and he's always protective of the one who is more vulnerable, who is actually supposed to be the master.'

'The three Wallace and Gromit half-hours are timeless,' muses Arthur Sheriff, Aardman's publicist. 'They're not set in a specific time. They can't be identified through what you see on screen as what's fashionable for that moment. They're timeless in themselves so something tells me that they'll always be around, and they'll always be reintroduced to a new generation and new viewers.'

Arthur also has an intriguing theory about why the films are so appealing, and so comforting.

'Each film starts at home and ends at home in the armchair drinking a cup of tea,' he points out. 'That's how Wallace and Gromit start and end their day. A very prominent psychologist told us that, to young kids, this is tremendously reassuring. They won't have nightmares of what happened in their adventures because it ends like this. There's a sigh of relief for a child who's been scared.'

But behind the characters and the plots, despite the comfort and the reassurance, there's something else. Something fundamental. The sheer skill and painstakingly hard work of one man – Nick Park.

Wallace and Gromit's home life has also been glimpsed through a variety of images specially composed and photographed for calendars, posters and magazine covers. Bristol's Great Reading Adventure – a collaborative project in the Bristol area to increase local literacy, used (amongst other things) an image of Gromit reading John Wyndham's SGF novel *The Day of the Triffids* whilst a large, carnivorous plant peered over his shoulder, whilst the *Radio Times* issue covering the period 29th August to 4th September had the two of them enjoying a sunny break by the sea...

'I don't use the word that often,' Kieran explains, 'but I think the *genius* of Nick is in the way that he managed to instil such believable character and such a great application of cinematic narrative style to the films.'

One example of that cinematic narrative style is the way that Wallace is totally oblivious to the fact that he's on TV, but Gromit seems to be aware that there's an audience out there watching his every move.

'In the *Thunderbirds* sequence in *A Close Shave*,' Kieran points out, 'when Wallace drops down into the saddle of his motorbike, Gromit comes in through the side entrance and rolls his eyes as he hops into the sidecar. And you just know that he's not doing it to Wallace, he's doing that to *us*. It's that "here we go again ... this is ridiculous" kind of thing.'

Bob Baker was equally impressed with the technical competence of Nick Park's animation in those early films. 'What it did show,' he says admiringly, 'was the total genius of the man: how those little nuances of movements and everything gave a special kind of life to his characters.'

One might expect Nick Park, who first created Wallace and Gromit and has steered their course ever since, to have the most to say about the characters of the pair of them, and why people love them so much. In fact, he has the least to say. Having shared his life with them for twenty years or so, he has the whole thing boiled down to one simple sentence.

'The way it works,' he says, 'is that Wallace is extrovert, and his dog is introvert yet a lot more intelligent. People can relate to that.'

And because people relate to it, because they love Wallace and Gromit so much, they want more than just the videos and DVDs and the occasional TV

A number of the Wallace and Gromit graphic novels were also published as strip cartoons in *The Daily Telegraph*, *The Sun* and the *Radio Times*.

repeat. In an attempt to sate this voracious appetite, several graphic novels and a storybook have, with Nick Park's blessing, filled in at least some of the details of Wallace's relatives, neighbours, schooldays and failed attempts to woo the fair Wendolene.

And when you've read all the adventures, why not expand your collection of Wallace and Gromit memorabilia. Over the years, a phenomenal range of stuff has appeared in the shops with their faces on: cufflinks, ties, socks, flannels, sponges, pyjamas, soap, food, car floormats… the list goes on and on to the point where most of life's luxury items are covered, in one form or another. And it's not just in the UK that you can buy Wallace and Gromit merchandise. Their appeal is pretty much across the board, around the world.

'I think Gromit, in particular, is very universal,' says Sean Clarke, Aardman's Head of Marketing and Licensing, 'because he doesn't speak and his mannerisms are global. Whether you're English or Japanese, you instantly recognize those humanesque features.'

Opposite bottom: A sign welcoming Nick Park on a visit to Japan.

'I remember,' says Kieran Argo, 'there was quite strong apprehension within the company when *The Wrong Trousers* came out. The question was whether it would actually translate internationally, but it did. For some reason it just struck a chord with a lot of people's perceptions of what Britishness is about. It didn't matter that they didn't necessarily get the subtleties of the Britishness, the British humour within the films; it just resonated with other people's perceptions of what Britishness is. And no more so than in Japan.'

'It's teenage girls in Japan that love Wallace and Gromit,' Lucy Wendover explains. 'They have a totally different view of them, a totally different view. They've interpreted the characters in a different way to us. They love them because they're quirky, because they're English ...'

This love of the characters has, on occasion, manifested itself in some strange ways. Lucy Wendover explains:

'I remember there was a Japanese documentary being filmed, and we had to find a family in Preston that they could go and visit, and have a cup of tea with. The family had to live in a house with flock wallpaper. The documentary must have had about ten minutes where the camera was just scanning over this wallpaper. They were just in raptures. It was incredible. And this family was just sitting there, like a typical English family, with the television on.'

Kieran Argo remembers a similar experience with a coachload of Japanese journalists.

'They came over on a big press junket – they actually shipped the journalists over here to see us instead of the other way round! The researcher who was in charge of getting their itinerary sorted wanted to see streets like West Wallaby Street; they wanted to go and meet people in Preston, they wanted to go and visit families in Victorian terraces in Preston, they wanted to see interior decorations like Wallace and Gromit's world ...'

This oriental fascination with Wallace and Gromit has resulted in a large amount of merchandise that's only available in Japan – much to the chagrin of collectors in the UK!

'We have an alliance with the number two insurance company in Japan,' Sean Clarke says, 'where they use the characters to promote their family insurance policy. When you take the policy out you get a range of gifts. They've done circular tables, little refrigerators ... Japanese products are fantastic, with their attention to detail.'

One avid UK collector of Wallace and Gromit merchandise did manage to get his hands on some of the items, however, as Sean Clarke explains.

'One of the promotional items we did in Japan was a folding Wallace and Gromit bike, which Nick Park now uses to get around the studio!'

Another example of the enduring popularity of Wallace and Gromit in Japan is the exhibition that has recently been touring around the country. Kieran Argo was intimately involved with setting it all up:

'About 1996/97 we started talking about doing an Aardman exhibition which relied very heavily on Wallace and Gromit material: sets, props and models, behind the scenes stills, images and a lot of information. It's a very common thing in Japan.'

'We had anything up to 40,000 people a week going through the exhibition,' Sean Clarke marvels. 'I think they like all the behind the scenes stuff as well.'

Kieran continues: 'They redeveloped the exhibition with a lot more Wallace and Gromit content, and they toured it around a number of top department stores throughout Japan. It was in Kobe, and Osaka, and Tokyo ... and it was hugely successful.'

But what is it about the exhibitions that attracts so many people?

'I think people do want to know,' Kieran muses. 'They want to get close, they want to be able to say, "I've seen a real Wallace and Gromit model", or they want to be able to see how the films were made, or the model making process.'

Although Japan remains the primary market for the big exhibitions, they have been displayed in other countries as well.

'We've had exhibitions in Arizona, in Boston. Malcolm Rogers, the director of the Museum of Fine Arts in Boston said they were more popular than Picasso!'

Holding the exhibitions does, of course, depend on there being enough material kept in storage from the original films to display.

With the full support of Nick Park and Aardman, a charity named Wallace & Gromit's Children's Foundation has been set up in order help improve the quality of life for children in hospitals and hospices throughout the UK. Their main focus of their fund-raising effort is 'Wallace and Gromit's Wrong Trousers Day' – an annual event in which people across the country swap suit trousers for clown pants and smart skirts for tutus to publicise the charity and to persuade the public to part with their cash.

'With *The Wrong Trousers*,' Kieran explains, 'there were only a few things that we managed to salvage. There was the museum set, which is a really nice piece and which is now residing permanently at the National Museum of Photography, Film and Television in Bradford. It's just under two metres wide by about a metre high and a metre and a half deep, so it's quite a sizeable set. One of the only other pieces that remains is Gromit's bedroom. We've had a few accidents along the way – sets have been damaged in transit. We tend to stay well away from using the original plasticine models because they just break up and get dirty, their fingers and heads fall off and the plasticine cracks. I usually have to get resin replicas made up of them. It's quite an expensive process, getting things looking right and being robust enough to tour around.'

Just in case anyone in the UK is feeling left out, plans are afoot to provide Wallace and Gromit's British fans with a taste of what the Japanese and Americans have already seen.

'We are developing a touring exhibition for the UK and beyond,' says Kieran. 'One of our potential partners for this project is @t-Bristol: a hands-on science centre in Bristol. We are also looking at ways of developing Wallace and Gromit in schools with inventing competitions and other activities.'

All of which derive, ultimately, from something that one young animator put together as part of his degree course. Wallace and Gromit have taken on a life well beyond anything that Nick Park envisaged for them, but he still has a strong interest in what happens to them.

'We're not like the big Hollywood studios,' says Sean. 'We won't go into certain product types if we don't feel they fit, even though they may make pots of money, you know. And we don't trying to influence the creative direction of the production.'

What is obvious to everyone at Aardman is that they are dealing with something of a very high quality indeed, and they are very careful not to do anything that might tarnish that quality.

'They are our crown jewels!' agrees Lucy Wendover. 'They are what Aardman are most well known for, and they are our most successful property in business terms. Looking at it from another direction, on a national scale, they are the most popular 3D animated characters that have come out of Britain.'

Above: A young fan reflects on his plasticine heroes at the @t-Bristol exhibition. Opposite: More views of Wallace and Gromit's adventures in the land of the Rising Sun.

The World of Wallace & Gromit

日本初、英国アードマンアニメーションズのアーチスト達の「手」が作り出す、
魅力あふれるストップモーションアニメの世界を一挙大公開！

Can I have a break?
The future for Wallace & Gromit

So what next for our intrepid heroes? They've been to the Moon, they've foiled a robbery, they've organized a jail break and they've cleaned the local grocers out of Edam. What more can life throw at them?

Opposite: A fun day out at the beach for the two companions.

The answer lies within the cavernous Aardman studios, located on a brutal industrial business park on the fringes of Bristol. For months, carpenters and electricians have been working away, quietly constructing the sets for a new project. A large project. An impressive project.

The Wallace and Gromit movie.

Originally entitled *The Great Vegetable Plot*, the film has now been renamed *Wallace & Gromit Curse of the WereRabbit*. Nick Park has been working on the script for a number of years now, originally with Bob Baker, who also co-wrote *The Wrong Trousers* and *A Close Shave* but more recently with colleague Steve Box, with whom he is also co-directing the film.

Wallace & Gromit Curse of the WereRabbit will mark Aardman's second venture into the cinema. Their first feature film, *Chicken Run* was a huge international success, meaning that a vindicated Aardman now feel comfortable enough to revisit their former glories and give the Great British Public what it has wanted for so long – a full ninety minutes of Wallace and Gromit on the big screen.

'Nick's ambition has always been to make a Wallace and Gromit feature film,' reveals David Sproxton, co-founder of Aardman Animations. 'That's why DreamWorks has hooked up with us, because they could see Wallace and Gromit were successful. And that's what we're working towards. The natural thing would have been to do it after *A Close Shave*, but after working with Wallace and Gromit for thirteen years Nick said, "Can I have a break?" He had reached saturation point. But while we were doing *Chicken Run* he was drawing Wallace and Gromit the whole time, because he always does!'

Security is tight, and nobody will reveal what the film is about, but sources hint that a close examination of the walls of Wallace's house in the three TV films might provide some clues as to some of Wallace and Gromit's cinematic escapades. And the title itself does give away a certain amount. All co-director Steve Box will say is, 'In the feature

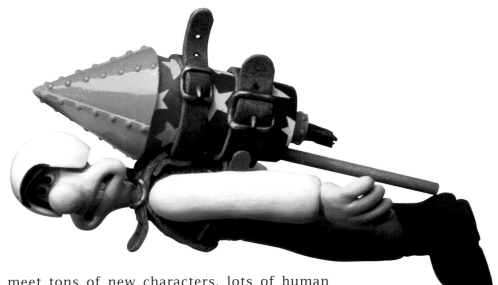

we meet tons of new characters, lots of human characters.' After that, his mouth is as sealed as Wallace's is wide open. Nick Park is equally circumspect. 'On the new film,' he says carefully, 'our main aim is to stay in tune with the originals.'

Should *Wallace & Gromit Curse of the WereRabbit* be as successful as history would tend to indicate, the expectation is that Wallace and Gromit's adventures would continue.

'We're now considering Shaun the Sheep as a stand-alone series for children, off the back of his success in *A Close Shave*,' Sean Clarke reveals. 'He was only in *A Close Shave* for five or six minutes, but was a hugely popular character. The new series uses very simple stop-motion animation, but it's getting a great response as a project and we haven't even presented animatics yet. People are so excited about it.'

Assuming the Shaun the Sheep series gets off the ground, it will be directed by long-time Aardman employee Richard ('Golly') Goleszowski. Golly has previously been responsible for such things as *Rex the Runt* and the new *Creature Comforts* series, and he's currently wondering how exactly to translate Shaun from comedy guest star to hero ...

'It's purely about sheep!' Golly explains. 'It's set in a kind of Wallace and Gromit type world, but it's just finding funny things to do with sheep. Sheep jokes! We're struggling a bit at the moment, because it's very hard working with scripts that have a lot of non-verbal communication. It's very hard to convey anything, apart from them looking quite blank and hoping that people will project emotion onto their faces.'

Aardman Animations are a pretty amazing company, Nick Park is a pretty amazing animator, and one of the most amazing things of all is the way two plasticine puppets, one of which doesn't get any dialogue, have taken the world by storm to the point where they are the central focus of a merchandising empire that spreads from the UK all the way to Japan and are about to star in their own movie. Of course, with Nick Park as a three-time Academy Award winner (twice for Wallace and Gromit and once for *Creature Comforts*) one can't help but wonder whether his talents might be recognized again for *Wallace & Gromit Curse of the WereRabbit*. Which raises a couple of important questions. If Wallace gets the Oscar for best actor, who goes up to collect it? And if Gromit gets the Oscar for best supporting actor, who gives his speech?

Credits

It's easy to picture Nick Park slaving over hot plasticine, alone in a small cubicle for hours, days and weeks on end, making the Wallace and Gromit films. In fact, as time has gone on Nick has been backed up by increasingly large teams of people, from other animators through model makers to musicians and production staff. Here's a list of the people who have also been involved in producing Wallace and Gromit's adventures:

A Grand Day Out

Animation and design: Nick Park

Additional model-making: Janet Sanger, Michael Hort, Michael Wright and Andrew Davies

B/W dream sequences: Joan Ashworth, Andrew Staveley and Martin Greaves of 3 Peach Animation

Special thanks to: Peter Lord, David Sproxton, Richard Goleszowski, Sara Mullock, Melanie Cole, Glen Hall and Alan Gardner of Aardman Animations

Thanks also to: Lesley Manning, Stephen Lawrence, Andrea Gardner, David Fine, Alison Snowden, Jeremy Clarke, Darren Long, Charles Paley, Cliff Thorne and Roy Swift; Triad Neg Cutters; Peter Bath of Technicolor; Harbutts Plasticine

Written by: Nick Park with thanks to Steven Rushton

Music: Julian Nott

Sound effects and sound editing: Adrian Rhodes, Danny Hambrook, with thanks to Chris Billing

Rostrum camera: Danny Boon and Jeremy Moorshead

Production: Soozy Mealing

Editor: Rob Copeland

Wallace's voice: Peter Sallis

Photographed and directed by: Nick Park

The Wrong Trousers

Animation: Nick Park and Steve Box

Additional animation: Peter Lord, Tom Gasek, Peter Thornton and Arril Johnson

Art Director: Yvonne Fox

Assistant Art Director – props: Ian Whitlock

Assistant Art Director – sets: Phil Lewis

Scenic Artist: Tim Farrington

Sets: Cod Steaks

Characters and props: Geoff Bevins, Trisha Budd, John Parsons, Jan Sanger and John Wright

Graphic design: Richard Higgs

Optical Effects Supervisor: Peter Wignall

Optical effects: Craig Chandler

Voice of Wallace: Peter Sallis

Production Assistant: Jason Marshall

Sound effects recording: Bill Morgan

Dialogue Dubbing Editor: Harvey Lilley

Trainee Assistant Editor: Tamsin Parry

Dubbing Editor: Adrian Rhodes

Dubbing Mixer: Aad Wirtz

With special thanks to: The Staff of Aardman Animations

Production Manager: Peter Thornton

Music: Julian Nott

Editor: Helen Garrard

Photography: Tristran Oliver and Dave Alex Riddett

Written by: Nick Park and Bob Baker, with additional contributions by Brian Sibley

Based upon characters created by: Nick Park

Executive Producers for the BBC: Colin Rose and Peter Salmon

Executive Producers: Peter Lord and David Sproxton

Producer: Christopher Moll

Director: Nick Park

A Close Shave

Voice of Wallace: Peter Sallis

Voice of Wendolene: Anne Reid

Key Character Animator: Steve Box

Character Animators: Loyd Price, Peter Peake, Gary Cureton and Nick Park

Assistant Animators: Sergio Delfino and Ian Whitlock

Floor Manager: Harry Linden

Art Director: Phil Lewis

Assistant Art Director – props: Trisha Budd

Scenic Artist: Tim Farrington

Set construction: Cod Steaks

Model Co-ordinator: John Parsons

Model Sculptor: Linda Langley

Model Makers: Jason Spencer Galsworthy and Zennor Witney

Model Technician: Del Lawson

Mechanical models: John Wright and Jeff Cliff

Photography: Frank Passingham, Tristan Oliver and Simon Jacobs

Camera Operators: Sam James and Paul Smith
Camera and Animation Assistant: Nick Upton
Gaffers: Ian Jewels and John Bradley
Animation Systems Engineer: Allan Yates
Technical Crew: Alan Gregory, Bob Gregory, Glenn Hall and John Oaten
Storyboard Artist: Michael Salter
Graphic design: Richard Higgs
Optical effects: Computer Film Company, GSE
Production Consultant: Peter Thornton
Assistant Film Editors: Tamsin Parry and Bridget Mazzey
Foley Artist: Jack Stew
Dubbing Editor: Adrian Rhodes
Dubbing Mixer: Paul Hamblin
With thanks to: Beth MacDonald, Toby Hannam, John McAleavy, Elizabeth Butler, Mike Booth, Susannah Shaw, Jason Marshall, Charles Copping, Douglas Calder, Adam Vernon, John Truckle, Tara Bacon, Darren Robbie, Ben Cook, Sophie Wright, Beverley Issacs, Curtis Jobling, Barry Shutler, Maxine Guest, Lisa Bilbe, Stuart Markovic, Janet Legg, Viv Paeper, Arthur Sherriff and the staff of Aardman Animations
Director of Photography: Dave Alex Riddett
Film Editor: Helen Garrard
Music: Julian Nott
Written by: Bob Baker and Nick Park
Executive Producer for the BBC: Colin Rose
Executive Producers: Peter Lord and David Sproxton
Producers: Carla Shelley and Michael Rose
Director: Nick Park

Wallace & Gromit's Cracking Contraptions

Voice of Wallace: Peter Sallis
Animation Directors: Merlin Crossingham, Andy Symanowski and Ian Whitlock
Animators: Terry Brain, Dug Calder, Mike Cottee and Darren Thompson
Assistant Animator: Maria Hopkinson Hassell and Alison Evans
Trainee Assistant Animator: Dan Ramsay
Story Artists: Michael Salter and Sylvia Bennion
Story development: Nick Park, Christopher Sadler, Lloyd Price, Steve Box, Michael Salter, Merlin Crossingham, Ian Whitlock, Andy Symanowski, Jay Grace, Seamus Malone, Peter Lord, Dick Hansom, Sylvia Bennion and Jane Kite
Model-Making Supervisor: John Parsons
Head of Model-Making Department: Jan Sanger
Sculptor: Lisa Newport
Props Supervisor: Jane Kite
Prop Makers: Jon Frier, Diane Holness and Neil Jones
Production Designer: Phil Lewis
Art Director: Matt Perry
Head of Art Department: Mike Applebee

Construction Manager – Sets: John Pealing
Construction Manager – Props: Ian Maccabe
Scenic Artist: Holly Beck
Set Builder: Mike Harvey
Set Dressers: Kitty Clay, Melanie Ford and Lois Garland
Set Prop Makers: Justine Bailey, Kathryn Williams, Duncan Miller and Martin Burnham
Director of Photography: Andy MacCormack
Lighting Camera: Jeremy Hogg and Toby Howell
Photography Consultant: Dave Alex Riddett
Camera Technician: Luke Smith
Gaffer: John Bradley
Electrician: Andy Loran
Floor Manager: Richard (Beeky) Beek
Model Rig Technician: Alan Barrett
Editor: Andrew Ward
Film Editors: Liam Owen and Dave McCormick
Title Design: Richard Higgs
Supervising Sound Editor: James Mather
Music Composer: Julian Nott
Assistant Sound Editor: Joseph Stracey
Line Producer: Harry Linden
Associate Producers: Sean Clarke and Carla Shelley
Executive Producers: Peter Lord and David Sproxton
Directors: Christopher Sadler and Loyd Price
Originated and produced by: Nick Park

With special thanks to everyone who helped in the making of these films

Wallace & Gromit Alive on Stage in A Grand Night Out

Wallace: Paul Filipiak
Gromit: Russ Edwards
Wendolene: Joyce Henderson
Shaun: Mark Otto Hollander
The Penguin: Angela Clerkin
Conceived and written by: Andrew Dawson
Inspired by the works of: Nick Park
Co-written by: Bob Baker
Designed by: Tom Piper
Lighting designed by: Jon Linstrum
Directed by: Martin Lloyd-Evans
Produced by: John Gore

Project Zoo

Bam Entertainment
Executive Producer: Marcus Fielding
Marketing Manager
International: Lia Tsele
Product Manager
International: John Merchant

Marketing Manager US: Kim Morgan

PR Manager US: Mika Kelly

Marketing Creative
Manager: Scott Baumann

European IT Manager: Paul Blakeway

Publishing Support Manager: Phoenix Valencia

Development Director: Joe Booth

Legal: Susan Young

Director of Business Development: Aaron Endo

Product Support Engineers: Jesse 'Mr Karate' Anacleto (Lead), Ken Barnes and Lance Page

TT123 Testing: Dave Hague, Tarl Raney, Duane Mortensen, Mark Collins, Bob Shink, Ryan Gibson and Jerry Pritchard

Frontier Developments Ltd

Director: David Braben

Producer: James Dixon

Story: David Braben

Script: Tristan Davies

Additional script: James Dixon and John Laws

Art Director: John Laws,

Music: Alistair Lindsay

Original concept & design: David Braben, Marc Cox, James Dixon and Jonny Watts

Level design: Steven Burgess, Laurence Oldham, Peter Parkin, Justin Rosewell and Tim Saunders

Cut scene direction: Gavin Gibbons, Neil Hall and John Laws

Intro and Finale: Gavin Gibbons, Neil Hall and Dean Stolpmann

Game programming: Tom Beckmann, Howard Chalkley, Steven Guest, Jon Travers, Stefano Bucciarelli, Tim Hughes and James Dixon

Engine programming: David Scantlebury, Robin Bryce, Tom Clapham, Jon Lewis, Trevor Page, Jonathan Roach and Sergei Lewis

Art and models: Marc Cox, Jeremy Kay, Ed Bright, Neil Pettitt, Tjaart Kruger, Dean Stolpmann, Gary Bickmore, Craig Chivers and Shafeq Rahman

Animation: Neil Hall, Richard Parke, Gavin Gibbons, Gerard Huke, Milan Medvec, Marc Cox and John Laws

Voice direction: David Braben

Wallace lip sync: Neil Pettitt

Sound effects: Steve Cowell and Alistair Lindsay

Main QA: Michael Brookes and Andrew Thomas

Representation: Jacqui Lyons and Marjacq

The World of Wallace and Gromit

Film festivals and awards

W allace and Gromit have won a number of awards over the years – usually accepted on their behalf by Nick Park. Here's a list of everything that's on the mantelpiece at 62 West Wallaby Street:

A Grand Day Out

Academy of Motion Pictures, USA (1990): Best Short Animated Film (nominee)

BAFTA, UK (1990): Best Short Animated Film

British Animation Awards, UK (1990): Best Film over 15 mins

European Licensing Awards (1996): Character Property of the Year

Golden Cartoon, Belgium (1991): (nominee)

Hiroshima, Japan (1990): Best Film over 15 mins

Zagreb, Yugoslavia (1990): Best Children's Film

The Wrong Trousers

Academy of Motion Pictures Arts and Sciences, USA (March 1994): Award for Best Short Animated Film

Atlantic Film Festival, Nova Scotia (December 1995): Children's Choice Award for Best Production Under 60 Minutes

BAFTA (British Academy of Film and Television Arts) (April 1994): BAFTA Award, Best Short Animated Film

BKSTS President's Award (1994)

Blackpool Film Festival, England (June 1994): Golden Tower Award

Cairo International Film Festival For Children, Egypt (September 1994): Golden Cairo for Cartoon Films

Chicago International Film Festival, USA (1993): Golden Hugo Award

Cinanima International Animated Film Festival, Portugal (1993): Grand Prize

Clermont-Ferrand International Short Film Festival (6th), France (1994): Public Prize; Press Prize

Cork Film Festival (38th), Ireland (1993): Special Jury Commendation

European Association of Animation Film, Brussels (September 1994): Cartoon D'or

European Licensing Awards (1996): Character Property of the Year

Festival du Cinema International en Abitibi-Temiscamingue, Canada (1993): Prix Anime

Festival International du Court Metrage, Montreal, Canada (April 1994): Distinction for the Excellence of the Entire Work

Hamburg Short Film Festival, Germany (May 1994): Audience Prize for Best Film

Hiroshima '94 The 5th International Animation Festival in Japan (August 1994): Best Film Category G

International Short Film Festival, Vila do Conde, Portugal (July 1994): Audience Prize

Krok Animation Festival, Ukraine (September 1995): Special Jury Prize

Mendrisio Cartoon '94, Mendrisio, Switzerland (November 1994): First Prize

Oberhausen Film Festival (1994): Children's Short Film Prize

Odense Film Festival, Denmark (August 1995): Jury prize

Ottawa Film Festival (1994): Grand Prix

PACT Indies Awards, London (March 1994): *Radio Times* Readers Poll; Best Programme; Best Music & Arts Programme

Seattle International Film Festival, USA (June 1994): Golden Space Needle Award for Best Short Film

Semana Internacional de Cine de Valladolid, Spain (1993): Special Jury Prize; Special Mention

Stuttgart Film Festival (March 1994): Award for Funniest Film; Audience Prize

Sydney Film Festival, Australia (June 1994): Audience Prize for Best Short Film; Film Critic's Circle Prize for Best Short Film

Tampere 24th International Short Film Festival, Finland (March 1994): Grand Prix; Audience Award

Umbria Film Festival (VII) (December 1995): Opera Nuova Prize Menzione Speciale cortometraggi

Vila do Conde, Portugal (June 1994): Public Prize

Zagreb World Festival of Animated Film, Croatia (June 1994): Grand Prix

Zoom! The International Children's Film festival. Toronto, Canada (March 1994): The Nelvana Award

A Close Shave

Academy of Motion Pictures Arts and Sciences, Hollywood, USA (March 1996): Award for Best Short Animated Film

Anima Mundi Animation Festival, Rio de Janeiro, Brazil (August 1996): Audience Award

Ankara International Film Festival, Turkey (March 1996): Second Prize

Annecy Animation Festival, France (May 1997): Audience prize

Aspen Shortsfest, Aspen Co., USA (February 1996): Animated Eye Award

BKSTS Technical and Scientific Award (1996)

British Academy of Film and Television Arts, London, UK (April 1996): BAFTA for Best Animated Film (1995)

British Animation Awards, London, England (February 1996): Best film over fifteen minutes; Best Scenario; Public Choice Award for Favourite Film; Public Choice Award for Funniest Film

Broadcasting Press Guild Awards 1995, London, UK (March 1996): Best Entertainment

Cairo International Film Festival for Children, Cairo, Egypt (February 1996): Bronze Cairo for Cartoon Films; The Children Jury's Prize

Chicago International Children's Film Festival, Chicago, USA: Outstanding Director Award, Best Animated Short

Cinanima'96 20th International Animated Film Festival, Espinho, Portugal (November 1996): Jury Prize – Class D

European Licensing Awards (1996): Character Property of the Year (1996)

Expo Cartoon – XX Salon of Comics, Rome, Italy (November 1996): Fantoche Prize

Fantasia Eta Beldurrezko Zinemaren Astea, San Sebastian, Spain (November 1996): Audience Prize for Best Short Film

Festival of Festivals, Arhus, Denmark (September 1997): Audience Prize

Goldfish, Russia (1996): First prize; Special prize for character

International Emmy Awards, New York (November 1996): Best Popular Arts Programme

International Festival of Films for Children (15th) ALE KINO!, Poznan, Poland (April 1996): Best Animated Film; Best Director; Main Children's prize for Art Direction; Judges Award for Supreme Contribution to Craft & Design

San Francisco International Film Festival, Golden Gate Awards, USA (February 1996): Certificate of Merit; Jury's Special Mention

Festival Du Cinema International en Abitibi-Temiscamingue, Rouyn Noranda (Quebec) Canada (October 1996): Prix Allime

Krok Festival, Ukraine (August 1997): Jury Prize

Montreal International Short Film Festival, Montreal, Canada (Quebec) (March 1996): PMT Video Public's Prize

Ottawa International Animation Festival, Canada (October 1996): Best Animated Production for Television; Special Jury Prize

Palm Springs International Short Film Festival, California, USA (August 1996): Best Animation (International); Audience Favourite Overall; Audience Favourite Animation

Portland International Film Festival, Portland, Oregon, USA (February 1996); Best Short Award

Royal Television Society Craft and Design Awards, London, UK (November 1996); Best Production Design; Best Sound

Stuttgart International Animation Festival, Stuttgart, Germany (April 1996); 'Pro-Sieben' Award

Tampere International Short Film Festival, Tampere, Finland (March 1996); 'Kiss' Statuette for Best Animated Film; Public Prize

Toronto Worldwide Short Film Festival, Canada (June 1997): Best Animation

Ulisees International Children's Film and Television Festival, Portugal (October 1999): Best Animation Over Twenty Minutes

Video Home Entertainment – The Awards of Excellence (1995): Top Programmes Animation

Vila Do Conde International Short Film Festival, Portugal (July 1996): Audience Award

World Animation Celebration, Pasadena CA, USA (March 1997): First Place – Best Stop Motion Animation

Wallace & Gromit's Cracking Contraptions

Cairo International Film Festival for Children (2003): Golden Prize for Best TV Programme; Children's International Jury Prize

New York International Children's Film Festival, New York (March 2004): Audience Award for 5–10 year olds

Acknowledgements

Thanks to Rachael Carpenter, Helen Neno and Kieran Argo at Aardman for organizing things so well; Nick Park, David Sproxton, Steve Box, Lucy Wendover, Debbie Smith, Sean Clark, Richard Goleszowski, Arthur Sheriff, Bob Baker, Dave Alex Riddett, Tristan Oliver, Marcus Fielding, Lia Tsele, Julian Nott and Andrew Dawson for their time and their humour; Helen Grimmett and Paul Simpson, for transcribing the many MiniDiscs so speedily and so fluently; Natalie Jerome and Jacqui Butler, for making the editing process so painless; Dan Newman, as usual, for his amazing design skills; John Catherall, David Owen, John Stacey and Andrew Caldwell for stepping in to prevent a nervous breakdown.

Additional thanks to Angie Last, Amy Robinson, Sarah Hodson, Janie Conley and all of the staff at Aardman, past and present who have helped bring Wallace & Gromit to life.